Principal Evaluation

Standards,
Rubrics, and
Tools for Effective
Performance

Principal
Evaluation

James H. Stronge

with contributions by
Xianxuan Xu, Lauri M. Leeper, and Virginia C. Tonneson

 Alexandria, Virginia USA

1703 N. Beauregard St. • Alexandria, VA 22311-1714 USA
Phone: 800-933-2723 or 703-578-9600 • Fax: 703-575-5400
Website: www.ascd.org • E-mail: member@ascd.org
Author guidelines: www.ascd.org/write

Gene R. Carter, *Executive Director;* Mary Catherine (MC) Desrosiers, *Chief Program Development Officer;* Richard Papale, *Publisher;* Genny Ostertag, *Acquisitions Editor;* Julie Houtz, *Director, Book Editing & Production;* Ernesto Yermoli, *Editor;* Georgia Park, *Senior Graphic Designer;* Mike Kalyan, *Production Manager;* Valerie Younkin, *Desktop Publishing Specialist*

Printed in the United States of America. Cover art © 2013 by ASCD. ASCD publications present a variety of viewpoints. The views expressed or implied in this book should not be interpreted as official positions of the Association.

All web links in this book are correct as of the publication date below but may have become inactive or otherwise modified since that time. If you notice a deactivated or changed link, please e-mail books@ascd.org with the words "Link Update" in the subject line. In your message, please specify the web link, the book title, and the page number on which the link appears.

PAPERBACK ISBN: 978-1-4166-1527-9   ASCD product #113025   n3/13
Also available as an e-book (see Books in Print for the ISBNs).

Quantity discounts: 10–49 copies, 10%; 50+ copies, 15%; for 1,000 or more copies, call 800-933-2723, ext. 5634, or 703-575-5634. For desk copies: www.ascd.org/deskcopy.

Library of Congress Cataloging-in-Publication Data
Stronge, James H.
  Principal evaluation : standards, rubrics, and tools for effective performance / James H. Stronge; with contributions by Xianxuan Xu, Lauri Leeper, and Virginia Tonneson.
    pages cm
  Includes bibliographical references and index.
  ISBN 978-1-4166-1527-9 (pbk. : alk. paper)
  1. School principals—Rating of.   I. Title.
  LB2831.96.S77 2013
  371.2'012—dc23
                                                    2012047021

23 22 21 20 19 18 17 16 15 14 13   1 2 3 4 5 6 7 8 9 10 11 12

Principal Evaluation

Standards, Rubrics, and Tools for Effective Performance

Preface

The purpose of this book is to provide guidance on the design of a comprehensive principal evaluation system that is grounded on the extant research and established best practices. The book is organized into three interlocking parts:

Part 1: How to Build an Evaluation System That Works. This section describes a conceptual framework for designing a principal evaluation system. It then moves to a detailed discussion of how to build such a system on a solid foundation of research-based performance standards.

Part 2: Comprehensive Set of Principal Performance Standards, Indicators, and Rubrics. This is the heart of the book. It provides a set of seven thoroughly researched and field-tested principal performance standards, including six that are based on the principal's work and one that is based on the results of the principal's work. This section also includes a solid set of "look-fors" (i.e., performance indicators) that describe what constitutes good work and how the principal is expected to perform it. Finally, each standard is attached to a four-point performance appraisal rubric for evaluating the actual work of the principal.

Part 3: Principal Evaluation Steps, Guidelines, and Resources. In this part of the book you'll find a selection of practical tools—including step-by-step design plans, guidelines for successful implementation, and a list of helpful resources—to supplement the principal performance evaluation system. These tools are intended to be used as needed when thinking about, designing, and implementing a quality principal evaluation system.

This book is written with two primary audiences in mind: district leaders who are mandating and implementing new principal evaluation systems, and principals, assistant principals, and other school-based leaders who will be evaluated by the system. In addition to these two groups, no doubt all of your relatives will want a copy for their birthdays!

In all seriousness, I do hope sincerely that this book proves to be of value to you as you continue the important work of providing quality leadership for our schools.

With best wishes,

James Stronge

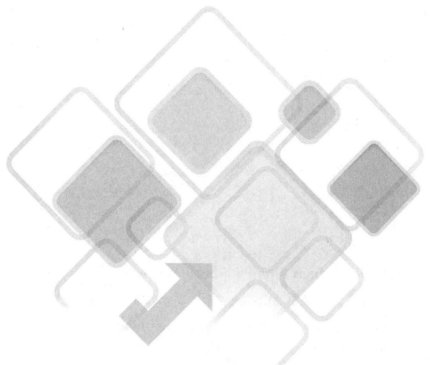

Part 1

How to Build a
Principal Evaluation System
That Works

Note: Select figures from this book can be downloaded at www.ascd.org/ASCD/pdf/books/stronge2013figures.pdf. Use the password "stronge113025" to unlock the PDF.

1

A Framework for Principal Evaluation

Ideally, a performance evaluation system for principals (or for any other educator) will affect the quality of teaching and learning and support ongoing school improvement. It's safe to say that documenting and improving the quality and effectiveness of a principal's leadership should be at the center of performance evaluation. Unfortunately, there is little connection between principals' evaluation results and the quality of their work. Although the disconnect between evaluation results and student learning has been much better documented for teachers than for principals, the same issue exists for both groups.

Without doubt, there are quality principal evaluation systems in place across the United States and around the world. However, too often, meaningful principal evaluation is the exception rather than the rule. We must reverse this pattern for two simple reasons: because quality principals matter, and because principal evaluation matters.

Principals Matter

Consider the following evidence regarding the role and value of the school principal in effective schools:

- "The experience of the DPS [Dallas Public Schools] is that the quickest way to change the effectiveness of a school, for better or worse, is to change the principal."[1]
- "The effects of principal leadership will occur indirectly through the principal's efforts to influence those who come into more frequent direct contact with students.... Achieving results through others is the essence of leadership."[2]
- School leaders are instrumental in facilitating professional learning communities focused on student learning.[3]
- "Principals of effective schools respect their teachers' skills and judgment, and allow them considerable autonomy in organizing and managing their classrooms. They also protect staff from excessive intrusion by forces outside the school."[4]
- Principals exert indirect influence on student achievement through their effect on school climate.[5]
- "The more school leaders focus their relationships, their work, and their learning on the core business of teaching and learning, the greater their influence on student outcomes."[6]
- Wise principals understand that they cannot reach instructional goals alone. In fact, principals who distribute leadership across their schools contribute to sustainable improvements within the school organization.[7]

- "Interestingly, when the studies that report positive findings are reviewed, only one mediating variable shows up with consistency as a significant factor interacting with principal leadership: school goals.... This function of the principal—sustaining a school-wide purpose focusing on student learning—does receive empirical support."[8]
- Principals of high-achieving schools expect teachers and students to meet the schools' goals.[9]
- Principals who focus on school improvement have more effective schools.[10]
- Principals of high-achieving schools communicate to all stakeholders that learning is the school's most important mission.[11]

The list of how principals make a difference in their schools (and more specifically, in teaching and learning) goes on and on. Every day—from the simplest to the most complex—principals matter.

Principal Evaluation Matters

If there is one lesson we can take away from international comparisons of top-performing education systems, it is that human capital—that is, people—matter. Teachers and principals, in particular, are essential for school effectiveness. Putting our resources into recruiting, hiring, developing, and keeping the best teachers and leaders is paramount for success. And here is why evaluation matters: Unless we have effective evaluation systems in place that accurately differentiate performance, we simply can't even discern whether or not we have effective principals. Furthermore, if we hope to improve principals' performance, we must be able and willing to provide honest, accurate, and meaningful evaluation feedback in order to identify areas in need of improvement and enable principals to make informed decisions regarding professional development to bridge the gap between current practices and desired performance. If designed and implemented properly, a principal evaluation system can play a fundamental role in guiding professional development and renewal, and ensuring that our schools are both excellent and accountable.

Ratings of principals suffer from the same problem of grade inflation that afflicts teacher evaluation: Most educators are rated as top performers. Many of the current principal evaluation systems do not allow for shades of gray—principals are rated as either satisfactory or unsatisfactory. And even in evaluation systems that allow for three-, four-, and five-point rating systems, the reality is that principal evaluation, on the whole, has not been differentiating, growth-oriented, or accountability-based.

Unfortunately, even though a principal's effectiveness is recognized as a vital factor in improving student achievement, schools rarely measure, document, or use effectiveness ratings to inform decision making.[12] As a result, it is difficult to distinguish among poor, average, good, and excellent principals. One comprehensive study of principal leadership evaluation practices in the United States indicated that although states and districts focus on a variety of performance areas (such as management, external environment, or personal traits) when evaluating their principals, they have very limited coverage of leadership behaviors that ensure rigorous curriculum and quality instruction.[13] The study also found that the usual practices of principal evaluation lacked justification and documentation of the utility, psychometric properties, and accuracy of their instruments.[14] Other flaws in the current principal evaluation process include

- An absence of meaningful and timely feedback to most principals;
- A lack of consequences of evaluation;
- An absence of clear communication of criteria and standard protocols;
- A failure to enhance principal motivation and improve performance;[15]
- Nonalignment of evaluation instruments with professional standards, which can produce role conflict and subsequent role strain as principals have trouble knowing what they should focus their attention on.[16]

Principal Evaluation in an Era of Accountability

The school principal's role has evolved rather significantly over the past few decades. In addition to holding the largely managerial responsibilities of the past, today's principals are expected to lead their schools, increase student learning, and help staff to grow professionally. In other words, the position of principal has evolved to reflect the necessity of both management and leadership roles. Though the responsibilities are many, effective principals can and do balance them.

The purpose of a quality principal evaluation system is to support the principal's growth and development while simultaneously holding him or her accountable for student success. Although principals have always been expected, at least implicitly, to foster student success, one striking difference between today's principal evaluation systems and those of even a decade ago is the explicit expectation that principals are responsible for improved student achievement. In fact, principal evaluation is now virtually synonymous with school evaluation.

Figure 1.1 depicts the two key components of principal evaluation in most U.S. states and in a growing number of countries.

The question that emerges in this new era of principal accountability is as follows: *How do we design and implement a performance evaluation system that is based on the*

FIGURE 1.1

Two Key Components of Contemporary Principal Evaluation

evidence of what effective principals do, is fair to both the principal and the school organization, and balances professional growth and accountability? One approach, and the one that I advocate in this book, is to base principal evaluation squarely on practical, research-guided performance standards that include a balanced measure of both the principal's behaviors and the principal's effect on the school. Such a set of performance standards, shown in Figure 1.2, serves as the basis for this book.

Clearly, the performance standards are overloaded in favor of principal behaviors. This imbalance is justified: It is through the principal's knowledge, skills, and dispositions that results are achieved. The more effective the principal is in terms of all six of the behavior standards, the greater the likelihood of producing more effective and sustained results.

Balancing Job Responsibilities with Performance Results

Although measuring principal behaviors (i.e., the first six performance standards in Figure 1.2) is central to a quality performance evaluation system, it no longer is sufficient. Simply stated, the work of the principal is expected to produce results. Standard 7—Student Progress—reflects the focus of evaluation on holding the principal accountable for student achievement. In fact, the Student Progress standard is valued by policymakers, legislators, and the general public to such a degree that it alone has come to encompass as much as 50 percent of the total evaluation of a principal.

FIGURE 1.2

Recommended Standards for Principal Performance

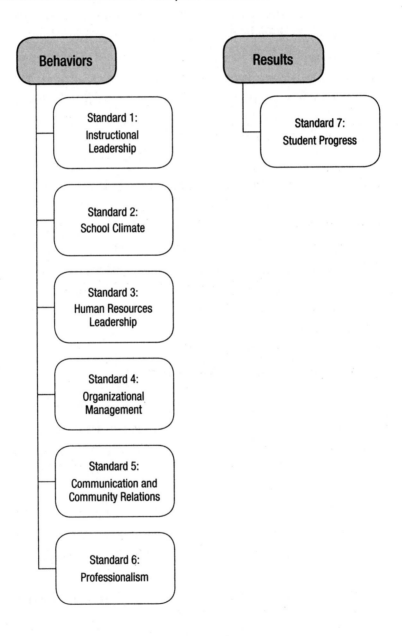

Figure 1.3 shows the typical weighting of behaviors and results in principal evaluation systems and the recommended weighting of the standards discussed in this book.

Example of a High-Quality Principal Evaluation System

One excellent example of a quality principal performance evaluation system is the one in place in Georgia's Gwinnett County Public Schools (GCPS). Just northeast of

FIGURE 1.3

Weighting of Performance Standards in Principal Evaluation

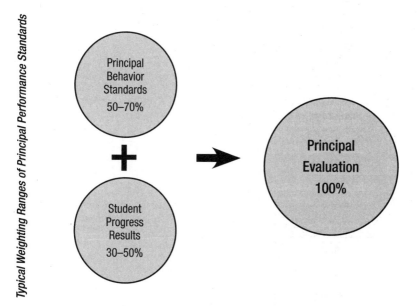

(Figure continued on next page)

FIGURE 1.3 *(continued)*

Weighting of Performance Standards in Principal Evaluation

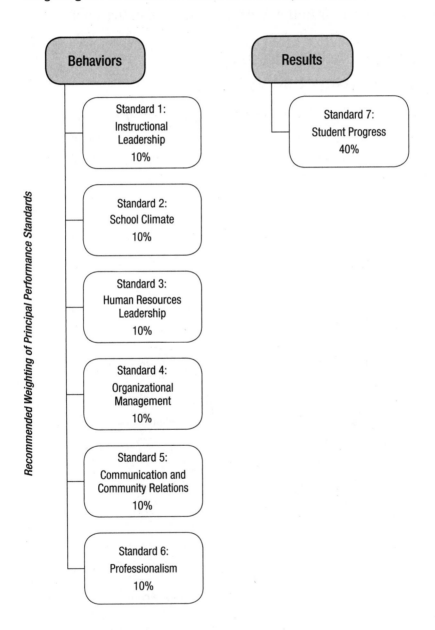

Atlanta, Gwinnett is the largest school district in the state, with 132 schools and approximately 163,000 students spreading across a growing and diverse community. For the past 10-plus years, Gwinnett has focused on quality in leadership. The school district boasts a comprehensive, homegrown leader development program; a thoughtful and careful principal selection process; and an excellent research-based professional development and renewal program for its leaders.

The district has also crafted a Results-Based Evaluation System (RBES) for measuring performance. In the RBES, individuals are held accountable for meeting an explicit set of performance standards articulated through key indicators that are explicit and measurable. The RBES is designed to meet specific and demanding requirements: to be fair, to provide accountability, to indicate individual strengths and weaknesses, to promote continuous improvement, and to support communication. The RBES is used to hold various stakeholders in the district accountable, including students, teachers, principals, support staff, district leaders, and the district superintendent. Components of the evaluation system include goals and rationale, baseline data, indicators of success, measurement methods and tools, an implementation plan, a midyear update, and a report of results and conclusions.

Gwinnett's effort to ensure quality evaluation for principals has played a prominent role in the district's success in recent years. Such success has not gone unnoticed:

- The district was selected as a finalist for the Broad Foundation Prize for Urban Education in 2009 and won the prize in 2010, earning $1 million for student scholarships.
- In 2011, the district was selected from over 90 school districts by the Wallace Foundation to participate in the Principal Pipeline Initiative, a $75 million initiative to establish strong principal "pipelines"—that is, local systems ensuring that a large corps of school leaders is properly trained, hired, and developed on the job. The key idea behind the initiative is that obtaining effective principals requires four essential elements: principal standards, high-quality training, selective hiring, and a combination of solid on-the-job support and performance evaluation, especially for new hires.
- The district was selected as a partner in the Bush Center's Alliance to Reform Education Leadership, which cited GCPS' Quality-Plus Leader Academy as an "exemplary program."
- In 2012, GCPS was featured in IBM's *Let's Build a Smarter Planet* series for its use of analytics to understand school performance and highlighted in a *District Management Journal* article ("Managing Principals for Results: Gwinnett County Public Schools").

GCPS has embraced the principle that excellent principals are essential for excellent schools. The district's model of evaluation speaks to its commitment to supporting principals and building the capacity of leaders.

Summary

The two major purposes of educator evaluation are professional growth and performance accountability, and there should be room in evaluation systems for both. Evaluation systems that reflect both of these purposes are not only desirable but also necessary for evaluation to productively serve the needs of individuals and the community at large.[17] In the current era of accountability, a practice-only view of evaluation is no longer enough; instead, what is needed is a practice-plus-results perspective. What the principal knows, values, and does is important, but so too is his or her ability to attain specific, observable outcomes.[18] The U.S. Department of Education has defined "highly effective principals" as those whose students achieve high rates of student growth (typically measured as one grade level and a half over the course of an academic year). The Department of Education also advocates for the inclusion of student growth as a significant measure of principal effectiveness in the evaluation process.[19] A strong nationwide movement for practice-plus-results principal evaluation is taking effect.

High-quality performance evaluation for principals, teachers, and all other educators must be the standard and not the exception. In this era of accountability, we must focus on growth-based, evidence-supported, results-driven evaluation systems that identify, support, and help sustain effective principals. This is our gold standard.

Notes

1. Mendro, 1998.
2. Hallinger & Heck, 1996, p. 39.
3. Reeves, 2006; Shellard, 2005.
4. Cotton, 2003.
5. Hallinger, Bickman, & Davis, 1996.
6. Robinson, Lloyd, & Rowe, 2008.
7. Hargreaves & Fink, 2003.
8. Hallinger & Heck, 1996.
9. Leithwood & Riehl, 2003.
10. Shen & Hsieh, 1999.
11. Cotton, 2003; Marzano, Waters, & McNulty, 2005.
12. Westberg, Sexton, Mulhern, & Keeling, 2009.
13. Goldring et al., 2009.
14. Goldring et al., 2009.
15. Reeves, 2005.
16. Catano & Stronge, 2006.
17. Stronge, 1995.
18. Clifford, Behrstock-Sherratt, & Fetters, 2012.
19. United States Department of Education, 2011.

2

Principal Performance Standards: An Overview of the Research

Coauthored with Xianxuan Xu and Lauri M. Leeper

To develop a comprehensive principal evaluation system that reflects the qualities of effective leaders, it is important to first examine the research base on what effective principals do. Figure 2.1 provides an overview of that research, divided into the six categories of recommended standards for principal behaviors discussed in Chapter 1.[1]

Following is an in-depth review of each of the six performance standards related to principal behaviors. Nearer the end of the chapter, we will turn our attention to the seventh performance standard related to student progress.

Standard 1: Instructional Leadership

The principal fosters the success of all students by facilitating the development, communication, implementation, and evaluation of a shared vision of teaching and learning that leads to student academic progress and school improvement.

FIGURE 2.1

Summary of the Research on the Qualities of Effective Principals

Instructional Leadership	
Principals of high-achieving schools have a clear vision and communicate to all stakeholders that learning is the school's most important mission.	*Sources:* Cotton, 2003; Marzano, Waters, & McNulty, 2005; Wagner et al., 2006; Zmuda, Kuklis, & Kline, 2004
Principals of high-achieving schools expect teachers and students to attain the school's goals, and they are confident that their schools can meet their goals.	*Sources:* Cotton, 2003; Leithwood & Riehl, 2003; Wohlstetter, Datnow, & Park, 2008
Effective principals understand that they cannot reach instructional goals alone, so they distribute leadership across their schools, which in turn contributes to sustainable improvements within the school organization.	*Sources:* Blase & Blase, 1999; Hargreaves & Fink, 2003; Leithwood et al., 2007; May & Supovitz, 2011; Supovitz, 2006
School Climate	
There is a positive relationship between school climate and leadership, which affects overall school effectiveness.	*Sources:* Barth, 2002; Hallinger, Bickman, & Davis, 1996; Leithwood & Jantzi, 2006; Marzano, Waters, & McNulty, 2005
Attempting to change the prevailing culture of a school is one of the more difficult tasks of the school leader.	*Sources:* Barth, 2002; Fullan, 2001
Relationship-building and stakeholder involvement are of fundamental importance in establishing and sustaining school success.	*Sources:* Cotton, 2003; Fullan, 2001; Kythreotis & Pashiardis, 1998; Wahlstrom & Louis, 2008
Human Resources Leadership	
Selecting capable and committed teachers is the core of the administrator's human resources responsibilities.	*Sources:* Fink & Resnick, 2001; Grissom, 2011; Marzano, Waters, & McNulty, 2005; Quint, Akey, Rappaport, & Willner, 2007
Effective administrators create a culture in which new teachers are supported and mentored by others in the building and the administrators themselves are critical resources of effective instruction.	*Sources:* Boreen, Johnson, Niday, & Potts, 2000; Mullen & Lick, 1999; Sweeny, 2001

FIGURE 2.1 (*continued*)

Summary of the Research on the Qualities of Effective Principals

Effective administrators provide the time, resources, and structure for meaningful professional development and recognize the teacher leadership within the building.	*Sources:* Blase & Blase, 1999; Cotton, 2003; Drago-Severson, 2004; Fullen, Bertani, & Quinn, 2004
Teachers leave the teaching profession for a variety of reasons, one of which is the lack of administrative support.	*Sources:* American Association for Employment in Education, 2000; Cheney, 2001; Hirsch, 2005
The number of teachers who are incompetent is much larger than the number who are documented as such, leading to a serious disconnect between reality and the ideal purposes of an evaluation system.	*Sources:* Menuey, 2005; Tucker, 1997
Teacher evaluation systems are integral to teacher improvement and overall school improvement.	*Sources:* Ellett & Teddlie, 2003
Teacher evaluation systems are integral to improvement in the classroom.	*Sources:* Duke, 1997; Howard & McColsky, 2001
Poor implementation and a negative atmosphere in which the evaluation takes place have caused teacher evaluation systems to fail in their purposes of improvement and accountability.	*Source:* Danielson, 2001
Organizational Management	
Maintaining a safe and orderly environment can affect teaching and learning positively and is therefore a fundamental responsibility of school administrators.	*Sources:* Bryk, 2010; Cotton, 2003; Lashway, 2003; Marzano, Waters, & McNulty, 2005; Shellard, 2005
Effective administrators make creative use of all resources—people, time, and money—to improve teaching and learning.	*Sources:* Cotton, 2003; Grissom & Loeb, 2011; King, 2002; Marzano, Waters, & McNulty, 2005
Effective administrators use multiple forms of data to inform school planning.	*Sources:* Cotton, 2003; Marzano, Waters, & McNulty, 2005; Shellard, 2005
Many administrative and organizational management tasks can be completed more efficiently through effective use of technology, allowing more available time for instructional leadership responsibilities.	*Source:* Buck, 2007

FIGURE 2.1 *(continued)*

Summary of the Research on the Qualities of Effective Principals

Communication and Community Relations	
An effective principal incorporates stakeholder views in a shared decision-making process and is a good listener.	Cotton, 2003; Leithwood, 2010
It is important for principals to engage in open and democratic dialogue with multiple stakeholders.	Leithwood & Riehl, 2003; Togneri & Anderson, 2003
Good communication is crucial to meeting school goals.	Marzano, Waters, & McNulty, 2005
Distributing leadership improves communication about the change process.	Waters & Grubb, 2004
Professionalism	
Effective principals are fair and honest, possess a high degree of integrity, and hold themselves to a high standard of ethics.	Lashway, 2003; Marzano, Waters, & McNulty, 2005
Effective principals communicate and model core values through their interactions with students and teachers. Most important, they model that they care for and have a genuine concern for children.	Cotton, 2003; DePasquale, 2012; Leithwood & Beatty, 2007
Principals who fail to perform their duties with competence and integrity and fail to cultivate relationships have low levels of trust in their schools.	Bryk & Schneider, 2002; Tschannen-Moran, 2004
Professional development that focuses on the roles and responsibilities as well as the nuances of context can positively affect a principal's decision making.	Leithwood, Harris, & Hopkins, 2008; Waters & Grubb, 2004

In general terms, instructional leadership is a focus on factors that promote and support teaching and learning.[2] More than ever, with the advent of stringent state and national learning standards, principals must concentrate on components that lead to student success and school improvement. Research indicates that instructional leaders do have an impact on student achievement, though indirectly.[3] Thus, it behooves principals to prioritize their instructional role as one of critical importance.

Effective instructional leaders focus their efforts on school improvement and student success. They do this by

- Creating a vision for the school community;
- Sharing leadership by distributing responsibilities, thus helping to create a cohesive team with a stake in successful outcomes;
- Leading a learning community by demonstrating the importance of continual staff growth and development; and
- Monitoring curriculum and instruction (see Figure 2.2.).

FIGURE 2.2
Instructional Leadership Responsibilities

Instructional Leadership			
Creating a Vision	Sharing Leadership	Leading a Learning Community	Monitoring Curriculum and Instruction

Creating a Vision

Effective, forward-thinking principals understand that creating a vision is at the heart of what they do—it is the impetus for all future goals, decisions, and dreams.[4] They also understand that for a vision to reach fruition, it must be inspiring enough to be embraced by others within the organization; it must become a shared vision.[5]

Principals of high-achieving schools are clear about their school's vision and goals.[6] A shared vision helps guide all in the school community to the ultimate destination: student success and school improvement. Because it is from the vision that goals for learning are established, buy-in to both the vision and the learning goals is important. The savvy principal understands this and seeks commitment from the school community.[7]

An example may help to illustrate the importance of shared vision. Providence–St. Mel is a high-achieving K–12 school serving an urban black population. Located on Chicago's West Side, 100 percent of its graduating students have been accepted to four-year colleges over the past 25 years. Researchers studying the school found that principals "worked hard to create a common vision of the school, one that definitely plays out in every classroom."[8] Teachers at Providence–St. Mel embrace both the vision and the learning goals that stem from it, believing that they are instrumental to the success their students enjoy.

Additional studies on high-achieving schools have found that they tend to have principals who

- Communicate to all that the school's most important mission is learning;[9]
- Believe that established school goals are attainable;[10] and
- Expect that both teachers and students can meet established goals.[11]

Sharing Leadership

Sharing leadership is not to be confused with delegating responsibilities or garnering extra help. Rather, it can be defined broadly as "teachers' influence over and participation in schoolwide decisions."[12] Effective principals understand the value of collaboration in successfully realizing the common vision. They realize that in order to meet instructional goals, they need buy-in from the staff.[13] By sharing leadership, principals acknowledge that everyone has important contributions to make and affirm the integral role that stakeholders play in helping the school to achieve its goals.[14] Capitalizing on the leadership and instructional strengths of other staff members is smart leadership: By helping to develop teacher leaders, principals strengthen their school's instructional program.

Principals who develop and tap the expertise of teacher leaders and refocus their emphasis on learning throughout the school improvement effort are more successful than those who do not.[15] Additionally, research indicates that tapping the expertise of teacher leaders can have the following benefits:

- Teacher leaders positively effect change from the classroom when they inquire about school improvement and then help to bring it about.[16]
- As teacher leaders work with principals toward school improvement, they provide valuable insights and ideas.[17]
- Teacher leaders willingly take on additional tasks and responsibilities that are not required of them but that benefit the school and other teachers within it.[18]

Leading a Learning Community

Learning is a lifelong process. Effective principals take the lead in promoting professional growth and learning for both themselves and their staffs. There are two primary functions around which schools are structured: (1) teaching and learning and (2) organizing for teaching and learning.[19] Communicating this focus to every stakeholder in the school community is a crucial responsibility of the principal.

Successful principals also prioritize student learning by paying attention to and communicating the importance of curriculum, instruction, and assessment.[20] One way they do this is by being visible in and around the school.[21] When teachers see principals out and about, interested in the daily goings-on, they see principals who are engaged and involved.

In order to promote the practices that lead to effective teaching and learning mastery, principals not only plan and organize professional development, they also participate in it—they become learners alongside their staffs. As Barth has noted, the principal as learner "is critical because there is a striking connection between learning and collegiality."[22] Effective principals recognize the value of collaborative participation in the learning community as a way to build trust and collective responsibility, and to further the goal of improved student learning.

Principals realize that keeping abreast of and informing staff about current research and practice are critical to school success. They emphasize and communicate that schools are learning communities, and they provide both formal and informal opportunities for collaborative learning.[23]

Research regarding the role of effective principals in leading the learning community concludes that effective principals

- Participate in learning alongside their staffs;[24]
- Ensure that learning opportunities are afforded to all staff members;[25] and
- Provide meaningful staff development.[26]

Monitoring Curriculum and Instruction

Effective principals focus on curriculum and instruction by monitoring teacher practice to identify instructional strengths and weaknesses. They are aware of instructional practices in their school buildings and are knowledgeable about the curriculum standards, ensuring that they are taught.[27] Additionally, they trust their teachers to effectively implement instruction, but also visit classrooms regularly to observe the results of that instruction.[28]

In effective schools, principals are able to judge the effectiveness of teaching and model expected behaviors.[29] By emphasizing teaching and learning, principals consciously limit activities that diminish instructional time.[30] They also allocate resources such as materials, staffing, and staff development opportunities based on identified needs,[31] and they encourage teacher reflection regarding instructional practices and their impact on student achievement.[32]

Research related to principals' roles in monitoring curriculum and instruction indicates that

- Both teachers and principals believe it's important that someone is positioned to guide the curriculum and make decisions about staff development needs;[33]
- Effective principals ensure continuity in the school instructional program;[34] and
- Principals must spend time in classrooms to monitor instructional programs, curriculum implementation, and the quality of instructional practices.[35]

Standard 2: School Climate

The principal fosters the success of all students by developing, advocating, and sustaining an academically rigorous, positive, and safe school climate for all stakeholders.

In general terms, school climate "is the relatively enduring quality of the school environment that is experienced by participants, affects their behavior, and is based on their collective perception about behavior in schools."[36] More simply put, school climate "refers to the social and working relationships of staff and principals."[37] When you enter the school's front office, how does it feel? As you walk down the halls, what behaviors do you notice? What is the energy level of teachers and students in classrooms? Does the school community work as a team? These and many other factors affect the climate in a school.

Because school climate affects everyone in the school community, enlisting the support of all stakeholders is an important first step on the road to establishing and maintaining a positive climate. And because school climate influences student outcomes, staff satisfaction, and overall school morale, principals should identify and implement practices that foster a positive climate (see Figure 2.3).

FIGURE 2.3
School Climate Responsibilities

School Climate			
The Principal's Role	The Stakeholder's Role	Trust	Shared Leadership

The Principal's Role

A positive school climate focused on student learning is correlated to student achievement.[38] Successful schools have a school climate that is significantly more positive than that of their less successful counterparts.[39] Because principals play a pivotal role in fostering and sustaining school climate, it behooves them to concentrate effort in this area.[40] To maintain a positive school climate, principals should

- Enlist the assistance of school community members (students, parents, staff, and community members) in helping to create a safe and positive learning environment;[41]
- Model respect and high expectations for all community members;[42]
- Share decision-making responsibilities to maintain high morale;[43]
- Maintain a current crisis-and-conflict action plan and implement it as necessary;[44] and
- Use knowledge of the social, cultural, leadership, and political dynamics of the school community to cultivate a positive learning environment.[45]

The Stakeholder's Role

Stakeholder involvement in school success is well-documented:

- Kythreotis and Pashiardis note that positive parent-school relations are among the 10 main factors in successful school leadership.[46]

- In a meta-analysis of school leadership research, Marzano and colleagues cite the building of professional relationships between school principals and staff as one of the critical principal responsibilities.[47]
- Cotton has identified parent and community outreach as an essential trait of effective principals.[48]

Effective principals, then, build positive relations between the parent and the school, build professional relationships with the staff, and provide outreach to parents and the greater community.

When applied to school principals, the adage "no man is an island" is most apropos. Collaboration, including shared decision-making responsibilities, strengthens rather than dilutes leadership capacity in a school community. Creating a positive and safe learning environment is a job for all— students, parents, staff, and central office personnel. Taking the time to build relationships paves the way for productive gatherings that move forward in the right direction. As stakeholders work to reach consensus around school norms and expectations, the savvy principal ensures that all voices are heard while at the same time never losing sight of the vision and school goals.[49] It is the responsibility of the principal to maintain both the focus on goals and the forward momentum.

The research surrounding principal and stakeholder involvement in school climate indicates that

- Principals possess the authority, power, and position to have an impact on school climate;[50]
- The effect of leadership on school climate in turn affects overall school effectiveness;[51] and
- Stakeholder involvement and relationship building are fundamental to establishing and maintaining school success.[52]

Trust

Trust is a precursor to success in any relationship, be it organizational or individual. If members of a school community are distrustful of others' motives and actions, that community will most certainly fail. Moreover, anxiety, isolation, and estrangement are correlated with the absence of trust.[53] The effective school principal leads from a position of trust—modeled and fostered daily in the school environment.[54] Principals desiring a trustful environment can cultivate one by sharing information, power, and decision making with teachers.[55]

Everyone in the organization benefits when trust abounds. Schools with high levels of trust are more open to new ideas and more likely to reach out to the community and commit to organizational goals.[56] Teachers demonstrate greater professionalism when principals demonstrate trust and when they adopt a professional rather than a bureaucratic orientation.[57] In schools led by principals of a bureaucratic orientation, control is often centralized and work processes are highly standardized. By contrast, in schools led by principals with a professional orientation, there is more flexibility, power is shared, and work processes are open to collective input and developed by shared decisions. Students are the recipients of higher levels of teacher trust when trust is a prevailing culture trait among school faculty.[58] Multiple studies indicate that increased collaboration, improved academic productivity, and risk-tolerant climates are positively associated with trust in schools.[59]

There are many facets of trust, including benevolence, competence, honesty, openness, and reliability.[60] Principals can demonstrate these qualities and inspire trust in others by

- Making the time to listen to others;[61]
- Asking for input from members of the school community;[62]
- Making decisions that foster student safety and achievement;[63]
- Being visible and participating in school activities; and[64]
- Supporting staff as both professionals and individuals.[65]

Shared Leadership

As the principal's role has evolved from a primarily managerial one to one that is both managerial and instructional, its duties and responsibilities have increased. To meet the demands of the job, it is increasingly necessary for principals to share leadership. Paradoxically, when principals give power away, they often become more powerful,[66] which enables them to narrow their focus and concentrate on factors that contribute directly to school effectiveness.

Shared leadership has been defined as "multiple sources of guidance and direction, following the contours of expertise in an organization, made coherent through a common culture."[67] In essence, shared leadership results in the creation of multiple leaders within a school. It affects principals and stakeholders in different ways: For the principal, it lightens the load and provides support; for the stakeholder, it highlights the important role that everyone has in guiding the school community toward its goals. When decision making becomes a team effort, the principal is more fully able to act as diagnostician and facilitator, identifying issues and the resources necessary to address them.[68] The principal does not relinquish responsibility, but rather promotes others, encourages shared decision making, and builds relationships.[69] All of these factors contribute to a positive school climate. The research also indicates that shared leadership has a positive effect on both reading achievement[70] and math achievement.[71]

Standard 3: Human Resources Leadership

The principal fosters effective human resources leadership by assisting with selection and induction, and by supporting, evaluating, and retaining quality instructional and support personnel.

In general terms, human resources leadership refers to the process of "selecting quality teachers and staff, inducting and supporting new teachers, mentoring novice teachers, providing professional growth opportunities, and retaining quality staff."[72] Surprisingly, many of the human resource functions performed in a school district take place at the school level. In fact, effective principals understand that one of their most important responsibilities is the selection, induction, support, evaluation, and retention of quality instructional and staff personnel.[73] They also understand that supporting and affirming teachers and staff while also finding opportunities for them to grow professionally affects the bottom line—student achievement.[74] Targeting the right people for the right position is critical, and effective principals take this responsibility seriously.[75] As Horng and Loeb note, "School principals can have a tremendous effect on student learning through the teachers they hire, how they assign those teachers to classrooms, how they retain teachers, and how they create opportunities for teachers to improve."[76] Figure 2.4 shows the four overarching responsibilities of human resources leadership.

A study by Beteille, Kalogrides, and Loeb found that principals' organizational management practices—particularly in the area of personnel management—appear to play a

FIGURE 2.4
Human Resources Leadership Responsibilities

Human Resources Leadership			
Selection	Induction and Support	Evaluation	Retention

critical role in improving schools. The study also found that effective schools retain higher-quality teachers and remove lower-quality teachers, and that teachers who work in more effective schools improve more rapidly than do those in less effective ones.[77]

Selection

Given that teachers have a direct effect on student outcomes, taking the time to make careful hiring decisions is worth the effort. This extends to the selection of support staff: One study by Portin and colleagues showed that principals were well aware of the impact support staff had on the climate of their schools.[78] Similarly, a study that focused on 90/90/90 schools—that is, schools in which at least 90 percent of students are minorities, receive free or reduced lunch, and get passing grades on standardized achievement tests—cited "mindful allocation of staffing resources" as a factor in the schools' success.[79] Additional studies indicate that principals trained in research-based hiring practices (e.g., multiple interviewers, prepared questions, scoring rubrics) are more likely to use those practices in teacher interviews and selection,[80] and that principals with a good grasp of their district's hiring system are particularly effective.[81]

Induction and Support

Quality induction programs have a positive effect on teacher retention.[82] As Wong notes, "*Induction* is the process of systematically training and supporting new teachers, beginning before the first day of school and continuing through the first two or three years of teaching."[83] Principals have an important role to play in fostering and sustaining these programs. With high teacher turnover rates showing no signs of abatement, the savvy principal provides as much systematic training and support to teachers as is needed throughout induction. Wong outlines the overarching objectives of induction programs:[84] easing the transition into teaching, improving classroom management and instruction, promoting the district's culture, and increasing the teacher-retention rate.

In a review of 15 research studies on induction programs, Ingersoll and Strong[85] found that beginning teachers who participate in them have the following advantages over those who do not:

- Higher satisfaction, commitment, and rates of retention
- More on-task students and viable lesson plans
- A greater likelihood of using effective student questioning practices and adjusting classroom activities to meet students' interests
- A greater likelihood of maintaining a positive classroom atmosphere and demonstrating successful classroom management
- Students with higher test scores or who demonstrate greater gains on academic achievement tests

In a review of the National Center for Education Statistics' Schools and Staffing Survey, which surveyed all beginning teachers in the United States during the 1999–2000 academic year, Smith and Ingersoll found three factors that appeared to reduce turnover rates for new teachers:[86]

- Matching mentors and mentees by teaching specialty (subject or grade level)
- Establishing a common planning time for collaboration
- Being part of an external network of teachers

It behooves principals to keep these factors in mind as they work to induct and support new teachers. Providing a culture of support where new teachers are supported by all staff can reduce new teacher attrition.[87]

Evaluation

The two major purposes of teacher/staff evaluation are professional growth and performance accountability. Though viewed by some as mutually exclusive, "There is room in evaluation systems for both accountability and performance improvement purposes. Indeed, evaluation systems that reflect both accountability and personal growth dimensions are not only desirable but also necessary for evaluation to productively serve the needs of individuals and the community at large."[88] Similarly, the National Education Policy Center advocates an evaluation system that "targets both continual improvement of the teaching staff and timely dismissal of teachers who cannot or will not improve."[89] An effective system meets both of these objectives.

If teacher evaluation is to benefit teachers, principals must consider ways to improve the evaluation process so that it is marked by quality characteristics, including

- A positive climate—that is, one "that fosters mutual trust between evaluator (representing the institution) and evaluatees holds the greatest potential for benefiting both parties";[90]
- Clear communication between teachers and principals, where both parties are encouraged and able to share ideas and interpretations, thereby fostering mutual understanding;
- A commitment to the process on the part of both teachers and principals so that the evaluation process becomes a vehicle for teacher growth and improvement. Principals can demonstrate their commitment by setting aside time and focusing attention on the evaluative process and by allocating resources that support both the evaluation system and teacher improvement practices;[91] and
- Technically sound practices, which require principals to participate in evaluation-system training.[92]

Research on these quality characteristics has shown that

- Teachers/staff who participate more fully in evaluation conferences are more satisfied with both the conference and the principal than those who participate less;[93]
- Principals who balance caring and high expectations build more trustworthy relationships than those who exhibit high caring and low expectations or low caring and high expectations. Balance is key;[94] and
- Teacher involvement at every level of the evaluation process is necessary for an evaluation system to be effective.[95]

Teacher/staff evaluation can also benefit from the use of multiple data sources or measurement tools to provide a more fully rounded picture of the effectiveness of those being evaluated. Moreover, the use of different measurement tools can offset weaknesses found in others. It is important to bear in mind that evaluation tools used without proper training can affect the validity of an evaluation.[96]

Teacher observation is the measurement tool used most often by principals during the teacher evaluation process. A study of measurement tools by Goe, Bell, and Little noted that although observations can provide useful information, their area of focus—instructional delivery and classroom management—is narrow, leaving such important aspects of teachers' work as instructional planning, student assessment, and professional development unexamined.[97] The National Education Policy Center advocates the use of multiple evaluation tools, including classroom observation, instructional artifacts, portfolios, teacher self-reports, student surveys, and value-added assessment.[98] When combined, these tools can provide a holistic view of teacher/staff performance based on both quantitative and qualitative data.

The research on evaluation suggests that

- School principals affect student learning primarily by hiring and supporting high-quality teachers and staff;[99]
- Effective principals hire, support, and retain good teachers while removing those who are less effective;[100]

- A principal's ability to perform evaluations affects his or her ability to remove teachers due to incompetence;[101]
- Remediating or removing low-performing teachers is the principal's responsibility;[102] and
- Effective principals continue to document deficiencies while working to help struggling teachers so that they have the necessary documentation should dismissal become necessary.[103]

Retention

Approximately one-third of new teachers leave teaching during their first three years of teaching, and fully one-half of them leave within five years.[104] Providing an induction program and support for new teachers has been shown to help keep new teachers in the classroom—a win-win strategy for all involved.[105] According to Marshak and Klotz,[106] mentors supported by principals help new teachers to

- Become familiar with the school's culture, traditions, and rituals;
- Learn more about the community's goals for education; and
- Gain insight into district and school policies and procedures.

Principals themselves support new teachers by helping them to

- Hone their instructional skills, such as learning to adjust delivery based on student need;
- Provide higher-level learning experiences;

- Develop the necessary skills needed to collect, analyze, and apply data instructionally to increase student learning;
- Integrate new technologies to enhance instruction;
- Engage in ongoing collaborative efforts within and among grade levels and subject areas; and
- Align their instruction with state and national standards, thereby ensuring that students are taught what will be tested.

Standard 4: Organizational Management

The principal fosters the success of all students by supporting, managing, and overseeing the school's organization, operation, and use of resources.

In general terms, organizational management pertains to those responsibilities relating to the functioning of the school. These include, but are not limited to,

- Coordinating a safe and orderly school environment, daily operations, and facility maintenance;
- Seeking and managing fiscal resources; and
- Organizing and managing technology resources.[107]

Organizational management is a primary responsibility of the school principal, and a smoothly functioning school requires a principal's focused time and effort. More than anything else, the school must first be a safe and positive learning environment for all—something school principals are charged to ensure.[108] Principals are also responsible for

- Using data to inform decisions and plan strategies for school improvement;
- Overseeing budgetary matters pertaining to the school; and
- Organizing and managing the school's technology resources.

If a school is to function efficiently and effectively, careful thought and committed time must be allocated to each of these areas (see Figure 2.5).

FIGURE 2.5
Organizational Management Responsibilities

Organizational Management

| Safety, Daily Operations, and Maintenance | Fiscal Resources | Technology Resources |

School Safety, Daily Operations, and Facility Maintenance

A school principal prioritizes student and staff safety above all else, creating and implementing routines and procedures that ensure a safe, orderly, and positive environment. In their meta-analysis of 69 empirical studies on school leadership, Marzano and colleagues identified "order" as one of 21 responsibilities of principals, noting that this responsibility encompassed such specific behaviors as establishing

- Routines regarding orderly school operations that are understood and followed by staff;
- Structures, rules, and procedures, provided and reinforced to the staff; and
- Structures, rules, and procedures, provided and reinforced to the students.[109]

Likewise, Cotton's research confirms that maintenance of a safe and orderly school environment is a priority of effective principals.[110] Cotton found that effective principals establish behavior policies developed with input solicited from staff and students. In addition, they

- Set clear expectations for student behavior;
- Ensure that discipline is fairly and consistently enforced;
- Grant teachers the authority to maintain the policies; and
- See to it that crisis management plans are in place, up to date, and supported by a trained school crisis management team that is on board and ready to handle situations effectively.

Principals complete a wide range of tasks on any given day, and even the most mundane of these can affect student outcomes.[111] For instance, heating and cooling problems can certainly affect classrooms and student learning. It therefore behooves the principal to keep the school running efficiently so that conditions are optimal for learning.

Master schedules, usually an administrative task, can affect student learning outcomes. Thoughtful and careful consideration while scheduling can result in more time for instruction.[112] Scheduling that maximizes blocks of instructional time and decreases "wasted time" is beneficial to all. Building in coteaching opportunities benefits students with special needs and others, as it effectively doubles teaching capacity. More needs can be met when principals include key personnel in the collaborative creation of a master schedule.[113]

Seeking and Managing Fiscal Resources

The school principal is charged with responsible management of resources. This requires a thorough understanding of local school board and state policy.[114] It also requires a cycle of actions to plan and oversee the budget. Resources include materials such as books and equipment, but also opportunities for staff development and professional collaboration.[115] Sometimes managing resources requires creativity to maximize teaching and learning. Research indicates that

- Effective school principals use resources creatively to improve teaching and learning;[116]
- Strong organizational managers allocate budgets and resources effectively;[117] and
- Schools showing academic improvement are more likely to have strong organizational managers.[118]

Organizing and Managing Technology Resources

As schools increase technology capabilities and applications, principals are expected to organize and manage those resources effectively. Principals must concern themselves with technology issues related to instructionally appropriate allocation, equity, sustainability, and training. To facilitate student learning and staff productivity, technology must be accessible and in working order. In addition, smart school principals hire technology staff who fully understand how best to capitalize on technology use for teaching and learning.

In a case study of 14 schools implementing technology use in both reading and mathematics, schools that achieved learning gains with technology were characterized by the presence of

- Support for implementation;
- A consistent instructional vision concerning how best to implement technology use;
- Principal support for scheduling access to equipment and collaborative planning time for teachers to learn about the technology; and
- Teachers' collaboration and support for one another on the use of the technology.[119]

Standard 5:
Communication and Community Relations

The principal fosters the success of all students by communicating and collaborating effectively with stakeholders.

In general terms, communication and community relations "consists of staff members' personal relations with colleagues, students, parents, and the larger community."[120] Communicating clearly and establishing strong relations with the community are critical school principal responsibilities. Increasingly, principals find themselves not only responsible to faculty, staff, and students, but also to parents, policymakers, and the larger community. Effective principals unite these various stakeholders into a cohesive group moving toward the same quality goal: educating children and raising student performance.[121] One of the ways they do this is through relationship building and savvy communications. Effective principals understand that they do not act in a vacuum; they realize the importance of bringing stakeholders into the mix in a collaborative decision-making model. Moreover, they reach out to stakeholders on a continual basis.[122]

Figure 2.6 shows the key principal responsibilities related to communication and community relations.

FIGURE 2.6
Communication and Community Relations Responsibilities

Communication and Community Relations		
Effective Communication	Communicating with Families	Communicating with the Larger Community

Effective Communication

Effective school principals foster communication with and among all school constituents on an ongoing basis.[123] They realize they do not have all the answers; they are good listeners and value the opportunity to hear alternate views on topics.

Today's technologies offer an array of communication possibilities and opportunities.[124] Porterfield and Carnes advocate the use of both traditional and new media to open the lines of communication and build trust with parents and the community. They offer five suggestions for improving communications:[125]

1. **Make communications planning a top priority.** Communication planning should be a consideration whenever new programs are designed, test dates changed, or rules revised. Principals should ask themselves (a) who should know about the changes and (b) how they can be assured that they learn about them. The answers to these questions ensure that all the affected parties are identified and a plan for communicating changes is in place. In other words, school principals should "get out ahead of the story, put your frame around it, and plan ahead."[126]

2. **Leave the office and network with others.** Networking builds relationships by increasing mutual understanding. It can take such forms as being available to news agencies, attending committee meetings of special groups (e.g., special education and gifted education

students), breakfasting with PTA officers, and meeting with faculty liaison groups. Such outreach demonstrates that the principal values these groups and is anxious to listen to their viewpoints and issues of concern.

3. **Be aware of the different audiences served.** School principals serve varied constituencies, each of which has different interests and concerns—they should not, therefore, lump all parents into one monolithic category. They also should ensure that employees are the first to hear of changes, that they hear the whole story, and that they fully understand the ramifications. Having done this, principals should enlist the staff's support in marketing changes to parents and community members.

4. **Invite naysayers to contribute.** Principals should look for those who find fault and enlist them in efforts to realize the school's vision. They should listen to their arguments and try to appreciate their views. When critics are invited in and become familiar with the school environment, relationships are built and new understanding is often forged. This is a way to become a team rather than adversaries.

5. **Use technology strategically.** Principals need to become familiar with how the community receives school information. For example, parents under the age of 50 often get news from online sources rather than printed newspapers. The school should survey parents to find out their preferred method of receiving information and focus communication efforts accordingly.

Communicating with Families

Principals who reach out to involve parents and community members and share the school vision with them are more successful than those who do not.[127] In a series of focus groups and a nationally representative survey of 1,006 parents of current and recent high school students from urban, suburban, and rural communities, Bridgeland and colleagues note that

- High-performing schools do a better job of communicating with parents and are more likely to be perceived as encouraging parental involvement;
- Parents of students in low-performing schools are much less likely than their peers to talk with their children's teachers; and
- High-performing schools are more likely than low-performing schools to notify and engage parents if their children are having performance issues at school.[128]

A review of existing literature on parental involvement found that the following types of involvement benefit the school directly:

- Telling parents that their involvement and support greatly enhance their children's school progress
- Fostering parent involvement from the time that students first enter school
- Teaching parents that they are role models for reading behavior

- Developing parent programs that are focused on instruction
- Working to engage parents of disadvantaged students
- Emphasizing that parents are partners of the school and that the school values their involvement[129]

Communicating with the Larger Community

It is the responsibility of school principals to "communicate a positive image of their schools."[130] To this end, principals should develop positive relationships with various media outlets and must "learn how to navigate the new digital ecosystem."[131] To accomplish this, schools might consider developing relationships with journalists, creating in-house news networks focusing on positive school outcomes, and connecting local stories to national studies and trends. Reaching out to the media strengthens school vision and develops relationships undergirded by shared purpose and mutual support.[132]

School effectiveness is in part influenced by a larger community network with which principals can partner to garner resources, enlist support, and form mutually beneficial relationships. Forming partnerships can assist in furthering the school vision to the larger community and can directly benefit students and teachers. One study of two Ontario secondary schools that were heavily involved in community partnerships found that benefits of partnering with outside agencies included

- The meeting of student and program needs that could not be addressed in the schools;
- Material, financial, and social support;
- Acquisition of district resources unavailable to other schools; and
- Enhancement of the schools' reputations within the communities.[133]

Standard 6: Professionalism

The principal fosters the success of all students by demonstrating professional standards and ethics, engaging in continuous professional development, and contributing to the profession.

In general terms, professionalism is defined as "the conduct, aims, or qualities that characterize or mark a profession or a professional person."[134] School principals set the standard for professionalism in the school building and the community. This includes demonstrating professional standards and engaging in ethical behavior. As role models for teachers and staff, they engage in continuous professional development and contribute to the profession.

According to Wurtzel, a professional

- Owes his or her primary duty to his or her clients;
- Is accountable to the profession for results;
- Has a duty to improve his or her own practice;
- Has a duty to improve common or collective practice in the profession;

- Adheres to a body of specialized knowledge, agreed-upon standards of practice, and specific protocols for performance; and
- Is expected to exercise professional judgment.[135]

Figure 2.7 shows the key responsibilities related to principal professionalism.

FIGURE 2.7
Professionalism Responsibilities

Professionalism		
Professional Standards	Ethical Behavior	Professional Development

Professional Standards

Compounding the increasing complexity of the principal's role are the various performance standards and guiding principles established by national, state, and local accrediting and governing bodies, some of which can contradict one another.[136] Leading performance standards for principals should support and complement the multifaceted role of school leaders. Consider, for example, the state of Virginia's standards for principals: The state's Uniform Performance Standards and Evaluation Criteria for Principals complement the 2008 Interstate School Leaders Licensure

Consortium (ISLLC) standards, and the standards of the Virginia Principal Evaluation System complement those of the Council of Chief State School Officers. When principals adhere to and demonstrate the professional standards set forth in the Virginia Principal Evaluation System, they can be assured that they are practicing professionalism and acting as role models to the school and larger community.

Ethical Behavior

School principals define and model their schools' moral purpose,[137] which can be defined as "social responsibility to others and the environment."[138] The principal's foremost responsibility to students, staff, and the larger school community is to behave ethically.

A survey of 180 K–12 educators found a correlation between effective leadership and ethical decision making. Survey respondents ranked honesty and integrity as the most important characteristics that educators value in principals.[139] Effective principals are fair and honest, have integrity, and are expected to demonstrate ethical behavior.[140] They share their ethical beliefs with faculty, staff, parents, and students.[141]

Professional Development

To hone skills and continue evolving in as highly skilled a profession as school principalship requires continuous professional development. One study that focused on why good principals stay in the profession found professional development to be key.[142] The principals surveyed viewed and described themselves as lifelong learners. Another study of 39 elementary schools whose principals participated in professional development found that

- The more professional development principals received, the more they were actively involved in the professional development of their teachers;
- Teachers who received more professional development taught lessons that were of higher instructional quality; and
- Schools where instructional quality was higher had heightened levels of academic achievement.

LaPointe and Davis found that effective principals are more likely than their less effective peers to

- Both attend professional development sessions and find them helpful;
- Engage in professional development along with their teachers;
- Make visits to other schools;
- Participate in development networks with other principals;
- Mentor other principals; and
- Be willing to observe and critique fellow principals.[143]

Additional research findings about professional development among principals suggest that effective principals recognize the importance of professional development,[144] and that research-based professional development programs providing what principals need to be successful are now available.[145]

Standard 7: Student Progress

The principal's leadership results in acceptable, measurable student academic progress based on established standards.

The six performance standards discussed so far reflect the empirical research regarding what principals should know and be able to do. However, in addition to a clearly delineated set of standards that comprehensively describe the key roles and responsibilities of principals, contemporary educational policy—and in a growing number of instances, statute—requires that principals be evaluated based on the *results* of their work. Thus, performance evaluation in today's educational world requires a new paradigm (see Figure 2.8). This process-results model holds true whether we are addressing principals, teachers, superintendents, or other educators.

In general terms, student progress is often equated with student academic achievement—that is, the academic growth of a student as he or she proceeds through the school years. (There are other measures of student success, but for our

FIGURE 2.8

The New Paradigm for Principal Evaluation

Process Standards *Principal Behaviors* →	Results Standard *Student Progress* →	PRINCIPAL EVALUATION

purposes, we'll stick to academic achievement.) Research in the field has consistently revealed that school leadership has an effect on student achievement over the years.[146] In a meta-analysis of research on the effects of principals' leadership practices on student achievement, Waters, Marzano, and McNulty found that the effectiveness of a school's leadership is significantly associated with increased student academic performance.[147]

Figure 2.9 shows the two main principal responsibilities related to student progress.

FIGURE 2.9
Student Progress Responsibilities

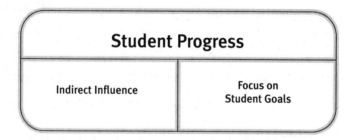

Indirect Influence

School principals "exert a powerful, if indirect, influence on teaching quality and student learning,"[148] often related to their influence on "those who come into more frequent direct contact with students."[149] Cotton has noted that principals of effective schools influence student achievement by

- Giving their teachers the autonomy they need in their classrooms to organize and manage as they see fit;
- Acting to ensure that instructional time is maximized by minimizing interruptions; and
- Focusing on student achievement.[150]

Simply stated, a school with strong leadership can have a positive effect on student learning, and a school with ineffective leadership can have a negative effect.[151] Research also indicates that school leaders can have a significant effect on student absenteeism, engagement, and academic self-efficacy, as well as on staff satisfaction and collective teacher efficacy[152]—all factors associated with student learning outcomes. Figure 2.10 shows data from an analysis conducted by Waters, Marzano, and McNulty regarding the effect of selected leadership practices on student achievement. Their research suggests that improvement in leadership effectiveness by one standard deviation can translate into an increase of 10 percentile points in student achievement on a standardized, norm-referenced test.

A Focus on School Goals and Student Progress

Using data on student progress to inform decisions helps leaders to formulate and attain school goals. As Usdan and colleagues have noted, principals "must collect, analyze, and use data in ways that fuel excellence."[153] Effective principals monitor progress, identify performance, and use the information to make program adjustments.[154] They also encourage their staffs to use data to inform instruction and

FIGURE 2.10

Principal Leader Responsibilities and Student Achievement

Leadership Responsibility	The Extent to Which the Principal...	Average Effect Size
Situational awareness	Is aware of the details and undercurrents in the running of the school and uses this information to address current and potential problems.	.33
Intellectual simulation	Ensures the faculty and staff are aware of the most current theories and practices and makes the discussion of these a regular aspect of the school's culture.	.32
Input	Involves teachers in the design and implementation of important decisions and policies.	.30
Change agent	Is willing to challenge and actively challenges the status quo.	.30
Culture	Fosters shared beliefs and a sense of community and cooperation.	.29
Outreach	Is an advocate and spokesperson for the school to all stakeholders.	.28
Monitoring/ evaluation	Monitors the effectiveness of school practices and their impact on student learning.	.28
Order	Establishes a set of standard operating procedures and routines.	.26
Resources	Provides teachers with materials and professional development necessary for the successful execution of their jobs.	.26
Affirmation	Recognizes and celebrates school accomplishments and acknowledges failures.	.25
Ideals/beliefs	Communicates and operates from strong ideals and beliefs about schooling.	.25
Discipline	Protects teachers from issues and influences that would detract from their teaching time.	.24
Knowledge of curriculum, instruction, assessment	Is knowledgeable about current curriculum, instruction, and assessment practices.	.24
Communication	Establishes strong lines of communication with teachers and among teachers.	.23

Source: From the working paper "Balanced Leadership: What 30 Years of Research Tells Us About the Effect of Leadership on Student Achievement," by J. T. Waters, R. J. Marzano, and B. McNulty, 2003, p. 4. Copyright 2003 by McREL. Adapted with permission.

provide training to ensure that they can do so effectively and efficiently.[155]

As indicated in Figure 2.10, a number of principal behaviors related to vision, such as establishing clear goals and fostering shared beliefs, were also associated with student learning. Waters, Marzano, and McNulty found the average effect size of leadership on student achievement to be .25. A similar meta-analysis by Robinson, Lloyd, and Rowe also found that various research-supported leadership dimensions influence student outcomes (see Figure 2.11).[156]

Summary

The school principal's role has evolved dramatically over the past two to three decades. Besides the largely management-related responsibilities of the past, today's principals are expected to lead their schools with the ultimate goal of increasing student learning while helping staff to grow professionally. What was once fundamentally a managerial role has evolved to reflect the necessity of both management and leadership duties. The principal evaluation system proposed in this book comprises a set of standards that reflect the qualities of effective principals and that specify expectations in each of the six performance areas with the ultimate goal of supporting principal growth and development.

It is important to understand, however, that principals exert both direct and indirect influences on schools and the people who work and learn there.[157] Thus, the framework of principal effectiveness should not only contain standards related to the processes of leadership, but also to the outcomes. Correspondingly, a fair and balanced principal evaluation system should be based on empirical research related to factors that positively affect student learning and, at the time, reflect the connection between leadership practices and outcomes.

FIGURE 2.11

Effects of School Leadership Dimensions on Student Achievement

Leadership Dimension	Meaning of Dimension	Mean Effect Size
Establishing goals and expectations	Includes the setting, communicating, and monitoring of learning goals, standards, and expectations, and the involvement of staff and others in the process so that there is clarity and consensus about goals.	.42
Strategic resourcing	Involves aligning resource selection and allocation to priority teaching goals. Includes provision of appropriate expertise through staff recruitment.	.31
Planning, coordinating, and evaluating teaching and the curriculum	Direct involvement in the support and evaluation of teaching through regular classroom visits and provision of formative and summative feedback to teachers. Direct oversight of curriculum through schoolwide coordination across classes and year levels and alignment to school goals.	.42
Promoting and participating in teacher learning and development	Leadership that not only promotes but directly participates with teachers in formal or informal professional learning.	.84
Ensuring an orderly and supportive environment	Protecting time for teaching and learning by reducing external pressures and interruptions and establishing an orderly and supportive environment both inside and outside classrooms.	.27

Source: From "The Impact of Leadership on Student Outcomes: An Analysis of the Differential Effects of Leadership Types," by V. J. Robinson, C. A. Lloyd, and K. J. Rowe, 2008, *Educational Administration Quarterly, 44*(5), p. 656. Copyright 2008 by the University Council for Educational Administration. Reprinted with permission.

To evaluate principals effectively, we need to understand what an effective principal looks like. By monitoring, analyzing, and identifying areas of strength and areas for growth within the six performance standards and by examining the effect that the behaviors associated with each performance standard has on student progress, principals and their supervisors can be assured that principal performance is continually enhanced and refined.

Notes

1. Stronge, Richard, & Catano, 2008.
2. Hallinger, 2005.
3. Cawelti, 1999; Cotton, 2003; Hallinger, Bickman, & Davis, 1996; Hallinger & Heck, 1996; Kythreotis & Pashiardis, 1998; Leithwood, Louis, Anderson, & Wahlstrom, 2004; Mazzeo, 2003, Mendro, 1998; Robinson, Lloyd, & Rowe, 2008.
4. Kearney & Herrington, 2010; Zmuda, Kuklis, & Kline, 2004.
5. Kouzes & Posner, 2002.
6. Leithwood & Riehl, 2003.
7. Kearney & Herrington, 2010; Stronge, Richard, & Catano, 2008.
8. Pressley, Raphael, Gallagher, & DiBella, 2004, p. 231.
9. Cotton, 2003; Marzano, Waters, & McNulty, 2005; Robinson, Lloyd, & Rowe, 2008.
10. Cotton, 2003; Robinson, Lloyd, & Rowe, 2008.
11. Leithwood & Riehl, 2003; Robinson, Lloyd, & Rowe, 2008.
12. Wahlstrom & Louis, 2008, p. 470.
13. Hargreaves & Fink, 2003.
14. Kearney & Herrington, 2010; Leithwood & Riehl, 2003.
15. Leithwood et al., 2004.
16. Reason & Reason, 2007.
17. Chew & Andrews, 2010; Muijs & Harris, 2006.
18. Harris & Muijs, 2003; Gehrke, 1991; Muijs & Harris, 2006.
19. Stronge, Richard, & Catano, 2008.
20. Kearney & Herrington, 2010.
21. Marzano, Waters, & McNulty, 2005.

22. Barth, 1985, p. 93.
23. Blase & Blase, 1999.
24. Prestine & Nelson, 2003.
25. Lashway, 2003.
26. Marzano, Waters, & McNulty, 2005.
27. Cotton, 2003.
28. Portin, Schneider, DeArmond, & Gundlach, 2003.
29. Fink & Resnick, 2001; Marzano, Waters, & McNulty, 2005.
30. Marzano, Waters, & McNulty, 2005.
31. Kearney & Herrington, 2010.
32. Cotton, 2003.
33. Portin et al., 2003.
34. Leithwood & Riehl, 2003.
35. Fink & Resnick, 2001; Pajak & McAfee, 1992; Ruebling, Stow, Kayona, & Clarke, 2004.
36. Hoy, Tarter, & Kottkamp, 1991, p. 10.
37. Stronge, Richard, & Catano, 2008, p. 17.
38. Hallinger et al., 1996; Hoy & Hannum, 1997; McLaughlin & Drori, 2000.
39. Lindahl, 2009.
40. Johnson & Uline, 2005.
41. Cotton, 2003.
42. Cotton, 2003; Harris & Lowery, 2002.
43. Fink & Resnick, 2001; Leithwood & Riehl, 2003.
44. United States Department of Education, 2006.
45. Kearney & Herrington, 2010; Piltch & Fredericks, 2005.
46. Kythreotis & Pashiardis, 1998; Marzano, Waters, & McNulty, 2005.
47. Marzano, Waters, & McNulty, 2005.
48. Cotton, 2003.
49. Marzano, Waters, & McNulty, 2005.
50. Kelley, Thornton, & Daugherty, 2005.
51. Hoy & Hannum, 1997; Lindahl, 2009; Marzano, Waters, & McNulty, 2005.
52. Cotton, 2003; Kythreotis & Pashiardis, 1998; Marzano et al., 2005.
53. Daly, 2009; Tschannen-Moran, 2004.
54. Tschannen-Moran, 2009.
55. Tschannen-Moran, 2004.
56. Bryk & Schneider, 2002.
57. Tschannen-Moran, 2009.
58. Tschannen-Moran, 2009.
59. Bryk & Schneider, 2002; Hoy & Tschannen-Moran, 1999; Tschannen-Moran & Hoy, 2000.

60. Tschannen-Moran, 2004.

61. Fullan, 2001; Kouzes & Posner, 2002.

62. Marzano, Waters, & McNulty, 2005.

63. Cotton, 2003; Marzano, Waters, & McNulty, 2005.

64. Cotton, 2003; Marzano, Waters, & McNulty, 2005.

65. Cotton, 2003; Portin et al., 2003.

66. Kouzes & Posner, 2002.

67. Harris, 2005, p. 258.

68. Portin et al., 2003.

69. Cotton, 2003; Marzano, Waters, & McNulty, 2005.

70. Hallinger & Heck, 2010.

71. Heck & Hallinger, 2009.

72. Stronge, Richard, & Catano, 2008, p. 36.

73. Hallinger & Heck, 1996.

74. Sanders & Horn, 1998; Sanders & Rivers, 1996.

75. Portin et al., 2003.

76. Horng & Loeb, 2010, pp. 66–67.

77. Beteille, Kalogrides, & Loeb, 2009.

78. Portin et al., 2003.

79. Kearney & Herrington, 2010, p. 65.

80. Hindman, 2004.

81. Peterson, 2002; Portin et al., 2003.

82. Ingersoll & Strong, 2011.

83. Wong, 2001, para. 10.

84. Wong, 2001.

85. Ingersoll & Strong, 2011.

86. Smith & Ingersoll, 2004.

87. Ingersoll & Kralik, 2004; Sweeny, 2001; Watkins, 2005.

88. Stronge, 1995, p. 131.

89. Hinchey, 2010, p. 16.

90. Stronge, 1995, p. 136.

91. Poston & Manatt, 1993; Stronge & Tucker, 2003.

92. Cotton, 2003.

93. Helm & St. Maurice, 2006.

94. Tschannen-Moran, 2004.

95. McLaughlin, 1990.

96. Stronge & Tucker, 2003.

97. Goe, Bell, & Little, 2008.

98. Hinchey, 2010.

99. Grissom & Loeb, 2011.

100. Beteille, Kalogrides, & Loeb, 2009.

101. Painter, 2000.

102. Painter, 2000.

103. McGrath, 2006.

104. Ingersoll, 2002; Luekens, Lyter, & Fox, 2004.

105. Ingersoll & Strong, 2011.

106. Marshak & Klotz, 2002.

107. Stronge, Richard, & Catano 2008, pp. 89-90.

108. Cotton, 2003; Marzano et al., 2005.

109. Marzano, Waters, & McNulty, 2005; Waters, Marzano, & McNulty, 2003.

110. Cotton, 2003.

111. Lashway, 2003.

112. Danielson, 2002.

113. Friend, 2007.

114. Stronge, Richard, & Catano, 2008.

115. Cotton, 2003.

116. Cotton, 2003; Marzano, Waters, & McNulty, 2005.

117. Horng & Loeb, 2010.

118. Horng & Loeb, 2010.

119. Means, 2010.

120. Stronge, Richard, & Catano, 2008, pp. 110–111.

121. Lashway, 2003.

122. Cotton, 2003.

123. Leithwood & Riehl, 2003.

124. Porterfield & Carnes, 2010.

125. Porterfield & Carnes, 2010, p. 34.

126. Neely, 2005, p. 24.

127. Catano & Stronge, 2006; Cotton, 2003.

128. Bridgeland et al., 2008.

129. Cotton & Wikelund, 1989.

130. Stronge, Richard, & Catano, 2008, p. 117.

131. Carr, 2011.

132. Leithwood & Riehl, 2003.

133. Hands, 2010.

134. Merriam-Webster's Learning Dictionary, n.d.

135. Wurtzel, 2007, pp. 32–33.

136. Catano, 2002.

137. Lashway, 2003.

138. Fullan, 2002, p. 15.
139. Kaucher, 2010.
140. Lashway, 2003; Marzano, Waters, & McNulty, 2005.
141. Beck & Murphy, 1994; Fullan, Bertani, & Quinn, 2004.
142. Boris-Schacter & Merrifield, 2000.
143. LaPointe & Davis, 2006.
144. Boris-Schacter & Merrifield, 2000; Kythreotis & Pashiardis, 1998.
145. Waters & Grubb, 2004.
146. Bamburg & Andrews, 1991; Brewer, 1993; Hallinger, Bickman & Davis, 1996; Leithwood & Jantzi, 2006; Leitner, 1994; Witziers, Bosker, & Krüger, 2003.
147. Waters, Marzano, & McNulty, 2003.
148. Mazzeo, 2003, p. 1.
149. Hallinger & Heck, 1996, p. 24.
150. Cotton, 2003.
151. Heck & Marcoulides, 1996; Leithwood & Jantzi, 2000.
152. Cheng, 1994; Griffith, 2004; Leithwood & Jantzi, 2000; Leithwood & Mascall, 2008; Pounder, Ogawa, & Adams, 1995; Ross & Gray, 2006; Silins & Mulford, 2002.
153. Usdan, McCloud, and Podmostko, 2000, p. 2.
154. Leithwood et al., 2004.
155. Snipes, Doolittle, & Herlihy, 2002; Togneri & Anderson, 2003.
156. Robinson, Lloyd, & Rowe, 2008.
157. Clifford, Behrstock-Sherratt, & Fetters, 2012.

3

Essential Components of a Principal Evaluation System

Clearly defined professional responsibilities for principals constitute the foundation for a comprehensive performance evaluation system. In fact, a fair and comprehensive evaluation system provides sufficient detail and accuracy so that both principals and their evaluators reasonably understand their job expectations. The goal is to support the continuous growth and development of each principal by monitoring, analyzing, and applying pertinent data compiled within a system of meaningful feedback.

The system that I recommend here uses a two-tiered approach to define the expectations for principal performance consisting of seven standards and multiple performance indicators. Additionally, principals will be rated on the performance standards using performance appraisal rubrics aligned with each of the seven performance standards. The relationship among these components is depicted in Figure 3.1.

FIGURE 3.1

Relationship Among Principal Evaluation Components

PERFORMANCE STANDARD

Standard 4: Organizational Management

The principal fosters the success of all students by supporting, managing, and overseeing the school's organization, operation, and use of resources.

PERFORMANCE INDICATORS

The principal:

4.1   Demonstrates and communicates a working knowledge and understanding of the state's public education rules, regulations, and laws, and school district policies and procedures.

4.2   Establishes and enforces rules and procedures to ensure a safe, secure, efficient, and orderly facility and grounds.

PERFORMANCE APPRAISAL RUBRIC

Highly Effective *In addition to meeting the requirements for Effective...*	Effective *Effective is the expected level of performance.*	Partially Effective	Ineffective
The principal is highly effective at organizational management, demonstrating proactive decision making, coordinating efficient operations, and maximizing available resources.	The principal fosters the success of all students by supporting, managing, and overseeing the school's organization, operation, and use of resources.	The principal inconsistently supports, manages, or oversees the school's organization, operation, and use of resources.	The principal ineffectively supports, manages, or oversees the school's organization, operation, and use of resources.

Performance Standards

Performance standards define the criteria expected when principals perform their major duties. The performance standards for principals are used to collect and present data to document performance that is based on well-defined job expectations. They provide a balance between structure and flexibility and define common purposes and expectations, thereby guiding effective leadership. The performance standards also encourage creativity and individual principal initiative. For all principals, there are seven performance standards (see Figure 3.2) that serve as the basis for the principal's evaluation.

Performance Indicators

Performance indicators provide examples of observable, tangible behaviors that indicate the degree to which principals are meeting each standard. These help principals and their evaluators clarify performance levels and job expectations—that is, they provide the answer to what must be performed. However, the list of performance indicators is not exhaustive, and the indicators are not intended to be prescriptive. It should be noted that indicators in one standard may be closely related to indicators in another standard. This is because the standards themselves are not mutually exclusive and may have overlapping aspects.

Using Standard 4 (Organizational Management) as an example, a set of performance indicators is shown in Figure 3.3.

FIGURE 3.2

The Principal Performance Standards

PERFORMANCE STANDARD NAME	PERFORMANCE STANDARD

1. **Instructional Leadership**

   The principal fosters the success of all students by facilitating the development, communication, implementation, and evaluation of a shared vision of teaching and learning that leads to student academic progress and school improvement.

2. **School Climate**

   The principal fosters the success of all students by developing, advocating, and sustaining an academically rigorous, positive, and safe school climate for all stakeholders.

3. **Human Resources Leadership**

   The principal fosters effective human resources leadership by assisting with selection and induction, and by supporting, evaluating, and retaining quality instructional and support personnel.

4. **Organizational Management**

   The principal fosters the success of all students by supporting, managing, and overseeing the school's organization, operation, and use of resources.

5. **Communication and Community Relations**

   The principal fosters the success of all students by communicating and collaborating effectively with stakeholders.

6. **Professionalism**

   The principal fosters the success of all students by demonstrating professional standards and ethics, engaging in continuous professional development, and contributing to the profession.

7. **Student Progress**

   The principal's leadership results in acceptable, measurable student academic progress based on established standards.

Evaluators and principals should consult the sample performance indicators for clarification of what constitutes a specific performance standard, but performance ratings should be made at the performance standard level, *not* at

FIGURE 3.3

Sample Performance Indicators

PERFORMANCE STANDARD

4. Organizational Management

The principal fosters the success of all students by supporting, managing, and overseeing the school's organization, operation, and use of resources.

Sample Performance Indicators

Examples may include, but are not limited to, the following:

SAMPLE PERFORMANCE INDICATORS

The principal

4.1 Demonstrates and communicates a working knowledge and understanding of the state's public education rules, regulations, and laws, and school district policies and procedures.

4.2 Establishes and enforces rules and procedures to ensure a safe, secure, efficient, and orderly facility and grounds.

4.3 Monitors and provides supervision efficiently for physical plant and all related activities through an appropriately prioritized process.

4.4 Identifies potential organizational, operational, or resource-related problems and deals with them in a timely, consistent, and effective manner.

4.5 Establishes and uses accepted procedures to develop short- and long-term goals through effective allocation of resources.

4.6 Reviews fiscal records regularly to ensure accountability for all funds.

4.7 Plans and prepares a fiscally responsible budget to support the school's mission and goals.

4.8 Follows state and local policies with regard to finances and school accountability and reporting.

4.9 Implements strategies for the inclusion of staff and stakeholders in various planning processes, shares in management decisions, and delegates duties as applicable, resulting in a smoothly operating workplace.

the performance indicator level. Additionally, it is important to document a principal's performance on each standard with evidence generated from multiple performance indicators, though not necessarily from all of them.

Performance Appraisal Rubrics

The performance appraisal rubric is a behavioral summary scale that describes acceptable performance levels for each of the seven performance standards. It states the measure of performance expected of principals and provides a general description of what a rating entails. The rating scale is used for the summative evaluation of all principals—it guides evaluators in assessing *how well* a standard is performed. Performance rubrics increase reliability among evaluators and help principals focus on ways to enhance their leadership practices.

Figure 3.4 shows an example of a performance appraisal rubric for Standard 4 (Organizational Management). Note that the "Effective" rating represents the expected level of performance.

Alignment with the Interstate School Leadership Licensure Consortium Standards

The seven standards outlined in this book are aligned to the Interstate School Leadership Licensure Consortium (ISLLC) standards (see Figure 3.5). Although there is no guarantee that ISLLC is absolutely on target, what this alignment does is provide a level of confidence that the seven standards are solidly founded on current policy regarding what principals should know and be able to do. If we are working from the same research base and conceptual framework, then it seems logical that the two would match.

FIGURE 3.4

Performance Appraisal Rubric

Highly Effective	Effective	Partially Effective	Ineffective
In addition to meeting the requirements for the "Effective" rating, the principal is highly effective at organizational management, demonstrating proactive decision making, coordinating efficient operations, and maximizing available resources.	The principal fosters the success of all students by supporting, managing, and overseeing the school's organization, operation, and use of resources.	The principal inconsistently supports, manages, or oversees the school's organization, operation, and use of resources.	The principal ineffectively supports, manages, or oversees the school's organization, operation, and use of resources.

Note: The "Effective" rating represents the expected level of performance.

Summary

Principal standards, performance indicators, and appraisal rubrics: These are the basic building blocks for principal evaluation in my evaluation system. In the chapters that follow, I will delineate how to

- Document the principal's performance;
- Rate performance; and
- Use evaluation results for principal professional growth and improvement.

However, it is essential to keep coming back to the three building blocks discussed in this chapter because everything else in the evaluation system relies on them.

FIGURE 3.5

Alignment of Performance Standards with ISLLC Standards

Performance Standards	Alignment with ISLLC Standards	
	Interstate School Leaders Licensure Consortium (ISLLC)	Research Base from *Qualities of Effective Principals* (Stronge, Richard, & Catano, 2008)
1. Instructional Leadership	Standards 1, 2, 3, 4, 5	1. Instructional Leadership
2. School Climate	Standards 2, 3	2. School Climate
3. Human Resources Leadership	Standards 2, 3	3. Human Resource Administration 4. Teacher Evaluation
4. Organizational Management	Standards 3, 6	5. Organizational Management
5. Communications and Community Relations	Standards 4, 6	6. Communications and Community Relations
6. Professionalism	Standard 5	7. Professionalism
7. Student Progress	Standards 1, 2, 4, 5	8. Principal's Role in Student Achievement

4

Documenting
Principal Performance

Coauthored with Virginia C. Tonneson

The role of the principal requires a performance evaluation system that acknowledges the contextual nature and
complexities of the job. In order to provide a comprehensive and authentic "performance portrait" of the principal's
work, it is important to use multiple data sources for documentation purposes. The use of multiple sources

- Increases the validity of an evaluation for any professional educator;
- Allows for differing documentation needs based on
  job responsibilities of particular positions (e.g., classroom teacher versus school counselor versus principal); and
- Provides for differentiation of performance for personnel at different points in their careers.

Multiple data sources are needed because no single source
can adequately capture the complexities of school leaders'
work. The proper use of them can dramatically improve the

utility of the evaluation system by ensuring better performance feedback, enhancing the validity and reliability of the process, and offering a more defensible basis for evaluation decisions.

Recommended Data Sources

Principals and their evaluators should discuss the specific types of data sources that will be used in the principal's evaluation as well as the expectations about their quantity and quality. Figure 4.1 lists an array of sources that can help to provide accurate feedback on principals' performance.

FIGURE 4.1

Recommended Data Sources

Data Source	Definition
Self-Evaluation	Self-evaluation reveals principals' perceptions of their job performance. Results of a self-evaluation should inform principals' personal goals for professional development.
Informal Observations and School Site Visits	Informal observations/school site visits provide information on a wide range of contributions made by principals and may range from watching how a principal interacts with others to observing programs and shadowing the administrator.
Document Log	Document logs provide documentation generated by principals as evidence of meeting the seven performance standards.
Climate Surveys	Climate surveys provide information to principals about perceptions of job performance. The actual survey responses are seen only by the principal, who prepares a survey summary for inclusion in the document log.
Goal Setting	Principals, in conjunction with their evaluators, set goals for professional growth and school improvement.

Self-Evaluation

Self-evaluation can help a principal judge the effectiveness and adequacy of his or her performance, knowledge, and beliefs for the purpose of self-improvement. By thinking about what works, what does not work, and what type of changes one might make to be more successful, the likelihood of making improvements increases dramatically.[1] Although I don't advocate using self-evaluation directly as a component of a principal's evaluation, the benefit that can be gained by helping principals target areas for professional growth should not be overlooked.

Self-evaluation forms may simply list the standard and ask the principal to reflect on areas of strength and of weakness. To encourage development, the forms may also include a section where the principal can list strategies for improving performance. Figure 4.2 shows an example of a self-evaluation form.

Informal Observation and School Site Visits

Informal observations and school site visits, applied in a variety of settings, provide information on a wide range of contributions made by principals. They may range from watching how a principal interacts with others to shadowing the principal and observing programs in action. Site visits provide an excellent opportunity for evaluators to discuss various aspects of the job with a principal, either in the form of a formal interview or in a less structured discussion. An evaluator may ask questions that help the

FIGURE 4.2

Sample Self-Evaluation Form

1. Instructional Leadership

The principal fosters the success of all students by facilitating the development, communication, implementation, and evaluation of a shared vision of teaching and learning that leads to school improvement.

Areas of strength:

_____

_____

_____

_____

_____

_____

Areas needing work/strategies for improving performance:

_____

_____

_____

_____

_____

_____

principal reflect on his or her performance, thus providing insight on how he or she addresses the performance standards. Such a discussion may also help the principal think through the artifacts that he or she might submit to the evaluator as proof of proficiency in each standard. In addition, the evaluator may use the principal's responses to questions to determine issues to further explore with the school's faculty and staff.

Evidence from informal observations and school site visits may be recorded in a number of ways. A form may simply list the standard and indicators with room for evaluator comments, or it may be focused more on helping the evaluator ask questions related to the principal's meeting of the standard. Figure 4.3 shows the type of questions an evaluator might consider asking.

FIGURE 4.3

Informal Observation or School Site Visit Form

1. Instructional Leadership

The principal fosters the success of all students by facilitating the development, communication, implementation, and evaluation of a shared vision of teaching and learning that leads to school improvement.

Suggested Guiding Questions/Prompts:

- What opportunities have you created this year for collaboration among teachers?
- How have you strived this year to improve the teachers' effective instructional practices associated with different subject areas?
- How do you make sure curriculum standards are taught by the teachers and mastered by the students?
- How do you monitor teachers' performance and provide constructive feedback to them?
- What types of teacher learning and development activities or programs have you participated in this year? What have you learned?
- How do you involve the expertise of teacher leaders?

Comments:

_____

_____

_____

_____

_____

_____

Document Log

A document log is an organized collection of work that demonstrates the principal's skills, talents, and accomplishments for the purposes of evaluation. It is similar in many ways to a portfolio, yet is typically more concise, containing a more confined collection of artifacts. Documentation provides evaluators with information related to specific standards and provides principals with an opportunity for self-reflection, demonstration of quality work, and a basis for two-way communication with their evaluators. A document log can confirm a principal's effort to demonstrate distinguished performance, continuing work at an effective level, or progress in response to a previously identified deficiency. Written analysis and reflection, as needed, about artifacts should be included in the document log to provide insight into the rationale for the events and processes documented in each entry.

An easy way to organize documentation is with a cover sheet that identifies the artifacts the principal is submitting as evidence toward meeting a particular standard (see Figure 4.4). A school district may wish to include a list of sample artifacts for a principal to consider, or simply provide room for the principal to list the artifacts being submitted.

Climate Surveys

Climate surveys are an important tool used to gather client information from teachers or staff regarding their perceptions of the principal's performance. One of the benefits of using climate surveys is that the data collected may help

FIGURE 4.4

Sample Document Log Cover Sheet

	Examples of Documentation	Documentation Included
1. Instructional Leadership	• School district goals • School improvement plan • Strategic plan • District improvement plan • Vision/mission/core belief statements • Staff evaluation grid • Leadership/school improvement team agendas • Building administrator responsibility chart • Professional goals • Master schedule • Student progress monitoring data • Schedules for students in the alternative education program • Project-specific summaries of a goal • Program development • Staff development plan • List of school committees and members	

the principal set goals for continuous improvement—in other words, they provide feedback directly to the principal for professional growth and development. The actual survey responses are tabulated, analyzed, and reported by the principal as well as summarized in the document log. Figure 4.5 shows a sample climate survey form.

Survey summaries also may be used to provide information to evaluators that may not be accurately obtained through other types of documentation. Typically, survey summary forms ask the principal questions related to the process

FIGURE 4.5

Sample Climate Survey Form

The principal...	Exceeds Expectations	Meets Expectations	Does Not Meet Expectations	No Basis for Judgment
1. Is interested in building a quality school which provides quality education.				
2. Maintains open lines of communication with employees.				
3. Visits my classroom or work space.				
4. Makes helpful recommendations to me for improvement of performance.				
5. Carries out the evaluation program as it is outlined.				
6. Uses judgment, creativity, and logical thinking in solving problems.				
7. Initiates change for the good of students and for the running of the school.				

of the survey (e.g., How many surveys did you distribute? How many completed surveys were returned? Were there any factors that may have influenced the results of the survey?), a short analysis of the survey results (e.g., What did teachers or staff perceive as your major strengths? What did they perceive as your major weaknesses?), and a reflection on the use of the results (How can you use this information for continuous professional growth?).

Goal Setting

One approach to linking student academic progress to principal performance involves building the capacity for principals and their supervisors to interpret and use student achievement data to set target goals for improvement. Setting goals focused squarely on student performance is a powerful way to enhance professional performance and, in turn, positively affect student academic progress. Principals can set individual goals for professional growth that are tied to school improvement and improved student academic progress or to the school's strategic plan. The goals can be customized for the administrative assignment. Typically, the goals will be reviewed with the evaluator at the start of the school year, and again both mid-year and at the end of the year.

A goal-setting form should allow the principal space to describe

- The school setting and any unique circumstances affecting the school community;
- The topic addressed based on learning achievement, school achievement results, data analysis, or observational data;
- What the current data show;
- What the principal wants the learners or program to accomplish; and
- The means for attaining the goal.

Figure 4.6 shows a sample goal-setting form.

FIGURE 4.6

Sample Goal-Setting Form

I. School Profile (Describe the school setting and any unique circumstances affecting the school community as a whole.)	
II. Content/Subject/Field Area (Describe the topic addressed based on learner achievement, school achievement results, data analysis, or observational data.)	
III. Baseline Data (Describe what the current data show.)	☐ Data attached
IV. Goal Statement (Describe what you want the learners or program to accomplish.)	
V. Means for Attaining the Goal	

Alignment of Performance Standards with Data Sources

The data sources described above provide different types of evidence of meeting the performance standards. As principals and their evaluators think through potential data sources, they should consider how each source aligns to each performance standard. A chart such as the one shown in Figure 4.7 may be helpful for this purpose.

FIGURE 4.7

Performance Standard–Data Sources Alignment Chart

Performance Standard	Self-Evaluation	Informal Observation/ School Site Visits	Document Log	Climate Surveys	Goal Setting
1. Instructional Leadership	S	S	P	P	
2. School Climate	S	P	P	P	
3. Human Resources Leadership	S		P	P	
4. Organizational Management	S	S	P	S	
5. Communication and Community Relations	S	P	P	S	
6. Professionalism	S	P	P	S	P
7. Student Progress			P		P

P = primary source, S = secondary source

Summary

A principal's job is complex and wide-ranging, making it necessary to use multiple data sources to adequately document his or her performance. Further, documentation of a principal's performance should be a joint effort between the evaluator and the principal, allowing for both to provide evidence of the principal meeting each performance standard. Careful consideration should be taken when deciding which data sources will provide the most accurate and useful evidence, and principals should be encouraged to analyze and reflect throughout the data collection process. In this way, a more accurate "performance portrait" of the principal may be obtained.

Notes

1. Tucker, Stronge, & Gareis, 2002.

5

Rating the Principal's Performance: Performance Appraisal Rubrics and Summative Evaluation

In the last four chapters, we have addressed two key issues: *What is expected* of the principal (performance standards) and *how to find out* if the principal is meeting those expectations (documentation). In this chapter, we will focus on a third issue: *How well* the principal is meeting expectations. I suggest that evaluators use performance appraisal rubrics to guide them in assessing and documenting to what extent the principal is meeting each of the seven performance standards based on their review of multiple sources. I recommend using a four-level rating scale to evaluate a principal's performance for the summative evaluation, thereby ensuring that the evaluation represents a preponderance of evidence. An example of the rating scale as applied to the Instructional Leadership performance standard can be seen in the excerpt from a performance appraisal rubric shown in Figure 5.1.

FIGURE 5.1

Sample Summative Evaluation Rating Scale

Performance Standard 1: Instructional Leadership

Highly Effective	Effective (Expected level of performance)	Partially Effective	Ineffective
In addition to meeting the requirements for Effective, the principal actively and consistently employs innovative and effective leadership strategies that maximize student academic progress and result in a shared vision of teaching and learning that reflects excellence.	The principal fosters the success of all students by facilitating the development, communication, implementation, and evaluation of a shared vision of teaching and learning that leads to student academic progress and school improvement.	The principal inconsistently fosters the success of students by facilitating the development, communication, implementation, or evaluation of a shared vision of teaching and learning that leads to student academic progress and school improvement.	The principal does not foster the success of all students by facilitating the development, communication, implementation, or evaluation of a shared vision of teaching and learning that leads to student academic progress and school improvement.
☐	☐	☐	☐

Comments:

_____

_____

_____

_____

_____

_____

_____

_____

_____

Summative evaluations should be completed in compliance with the applicable state code and policy, and local school district policies and procedures. Once ratings are assigned, the results of the evaluation always should be reviewed and discussed with the principal at a summative evaluation conference.

Calculating a Cumulative Summative Evaluation Score

A growing number of states and school districts are requiring that a single summative rating be calculated and applied to principal evaluation. In order to calculate a cumulative rating, individual summative ratings first must be applied. Then, the rating for each of the seven performance standards can be weighted and considered additive, with the most significant weight given to Standard 7 (Student Progress). One option is to weight each of the first six standards at 10 percent each and Standard 7 at 40 percent. Of course, the actual weightings will vary, depending on state or local policy. Once a determination on the weight of each standard has been made, a decision needs to be made on how much each rating level is worth. One way of doing this is simply to make each rating worth a certain amount of points, as follows:

- Ineffective = 1 point
- Partially Effective = 2 points
- Effective = 3 points
- Highly Effective = 4 points

Figure 5.2 shows two examples of weighted calculations for arriving at cumulative summative scores using this point system. It is important to note that the use of point values such as those described here is based on policy guidelines that are becoming prevalent across many U.S. states. Because these point values are based more on a logic model than on the research base, the computations and applications of the processes for cumulative summative ratings are likely to undergo careful scrutiny and revisions over the coming years.

Applying an Overall Summative Rating

After the cumulative summative score has been calculated, a single overall summative rating may be determined. It is important for school districts to establish and document cut-off scores for the overall rating ahead of time. School districts may decide to use ranges of scores and standard rounding rules, such as determining that cumulative summative scores from 35 to 40 result in a single overall summative rating of Effective. Figure 5.3 shows an example of possible cut-off scores for the overall rating. Using the score ranges in this figure, the principal in the first example in Figure 5.2, who received a cumulative summative score of 36, would have an overall summative rating of Highly Effective, and the principal in the second example, who received a score of 28, would have an overall summative rating of Effective.

School districts also may establish and document additional criteria for the overall summative rating. For example, a

FIGURE 5.2

Examples of Weighted Calculations for Cumulative Summative Principal Performance Evaluation Scores

Example 1

Principal Performance Standard	Performance Rating	Point Value	Weight	Weighted Total (Point Value x Weight)
Standard 1	Highly Effective	4	10 (or 10%)	4
Standard 2	Effective	3	10 (or 10%)	3
Standard 3	Effective	3	10 (or 10%)	3
Standard 4	Effective	3	10 (or 10%)	3
Standard 5	Effective	3	10 (or 10%)	3
Standard 6	Highly Effective	4	10 (or 10%)	4
Standard 7	Highly Effective	4	40 (or 40%)	16
Cumulative Summative Score				36

Example 2

Principal Performance Standard	Performance Rating	Point Value	Weight	Weighted Total (Point Value x Weight)
Standard 1	Effective	3	10 (or 10%)	3
Standard 2	Partially Effective	2	10 (or 10%)	2
Standard 3	Effective	2	10 (or 10%)	3
Standard 4	Effective	3	10 (or 10%)	3
Standard 5	Effective	3	10 (or 10%)	3
Standard 6	Partially Effective	2	10 (or 10%)	2
Standard 7	Effective	3	40 (or 40%)	12
Cumulative Summative Score				28

school district may decide that no principals can be given a summative rating of Highly Effective if they are rated below Effective on any of the seven standards. Likewise, school districts may determine that summative criteria should differ for principals at different points on the career ladder. For example, they may determine that regardless of the cumulative summative score, principals with five or more years of experience who do not have a Highly Effective rating on Standard 7 (Student Progress) may not be given an overall Highly Effective rating. It would also be plausible to require that a principal with at least one (or perhaps two) Ineffective ratings from among the seven performance standards be rated as Ineffective for the cumulative score, regardless of the actual total point value. In any event, decisions about arriving at ratings and applicable documentation must be made before a new evaluation system is put in place, and it is critical that principals understand the requirements before the evaluation cycle begins.

FIGURE 5.3
Possible Score Ranges for Overall Summative Ratings

Score Range	Rating
10–19	Ineffective
20–26	Partially Effective
27–34	Effective
35–40	Highly Effective

Summary

The rating for each performance standard is based on multiple sources of information and is completed only after pertinent data from all sources have been analyzed. Performance appraisal rubrics are effective tools for facilitating the rating process. Among their advantages, rubrics

- Make assessing principal performance quick and efficient;
- Help evaluators justify the ratings they assign to principals;
- Reflect a logic model and are often self-explanatory—they should make sense at a glance to both the evaluators and the principals being evaluated;
- Clarify the expectations for principal performance;
- Make the evaluation process fairer and more transparent—evaluators no longer keep the criteria and standards to themselves;
- Ensure consistency and reliability among evaluators as they assess how well a standard is performed;
- Enable evaluators to acknowledge two levels of effective performance (i.e., Highly Effective and Effective) and two levels for principals not meeting expectations (i.e., Partially Effective and Ineffective), thereby providing principals with ample diagnostic feedback about their strengths and areas in need of improvement. This helps principals to focus on ways to enhance their leadership practices.

Despite improved fairness and objectivity, rating a principal's performance with rubrics is not a fine science; there still will be a degree of subjectivity in judgment. Two ways to improve the trustworthiness of evaluators' ratings are (1) establishing inter-rater agreement among evaluators and (2) ensuring all ratings are based on solid evidence of principal performance.

6

Implementing a Quality Principal Evaluation System

This chapter addresses the key characteristics of a quality principal evaluation system, ways in which evaluation results can be used to improve principal performance, and frequently asked questions related to principal evaluation.

Key Characteristics of a Quality Principal Evaluation System

A quality principal evaluation system should incorporate the following key characteristics:

- Adaptability
- A systematic approach
- An emphasis on communication
- Technical and conceptual soundness
- Use of multiple data sources

Adaptability

In order for an evaluation system to be uniform in design and implementation, it should be both comprehensive and adaptable for use with a variety of educational positions, not just principals. This can be achieved by

- Ensuring a uniform design for evaluating all personnel;
- Customizing the evaluation system to account for unique performance standards, data sources, and procedures for the specific target audience; and
- Designing processes that account for educators' different levels of professional growth (e.g., novice, advanced).

A Systematic Approach

It is not feasible for evaluators to implement multiple evaluation systems for different groups that feature discrete requirements, guidelines, and methods. Rather, to the degree possible, an efficient, standardized method for implementing evaluation should be considered. Although forms and processes will necessarily be differentiated from profession to profession, the evaluation model and protocols can be standardized. Standardization of the evaluation framework coupled with customization where necessary for the position being evaluated makes an evaluation system easier to implement while also accounting for distinctions in the roles and responsibilities of different positions.

An Emphasis on Communication

The evaluation system should reflect the fundamental role that effective communication plays in every aspect of the process. Because the goal of any evaluation is either to ensure that successful job performance continues or to

improve less successful performance, effective communication between the evaluator and the principal is essential.

Technical and Conceptual Soundness

Although technical and conceptual soundness does not
absolutely guarantee that an evaluation system will be effective, a flawed and irrational model does guarantee failure.
Thus, any evaluation system should

- Provide effective service to learners and society;
- Be constructive and free of unnecessary threatening
  or demoralizing characteristics; and
- Facilitate planning for sound professional development experiences.[1]

Use of Multiple Data Sources

No single data source can capture the complexities of
the work principals do. The use of multiple data sources
increases validity and reliability of the evaluation system by
accounting for the principal's various responsibilities and
helping evaluators differentiate among principals at different stages of their careers. Thus, multiple data sources offer
both the potential for better performance feedback and a
more defensible basis for evaluation decisions.

Using Evaluation Results to
Improve Principal Performance

Supporting principals is essential to the success of both
principals and schools. To ensure that evaluation is a

value-driven and growth-oriented learning process, I suggest organizing the practice around the following five guiding tenets:

1. **Numbers alone don't matter.** Simply fulfilling a policy mandate and applying a number to principals—or to anyone—reflects a sterile approach. The value of an evaluation comes from what we do with the results.

2. **Evaluation is not about "getting" underperforming principals.** There easily can be a mindset that we evaluate in order to identify who is ineffective and then use the evaluation results to justify personnel actions. Not so. First, second, and last, our aim should be to support, improve, and sustain quality principal work. When we use evaluation as a lever for quality control and quality growth, we get the best results.

3. **Evaluation is designed for *all* principals.** Without a doubt, we must deal with ineffective principals—sometimes, we might even have to remove them. However, evaluation is best when focused on growing and supporting *all* principals, including the vast majority of capable, competent, committed principals who populate our schools. In fact, evaluation should be designed so that all principals receive valid, constructive feedback to help them maximize their leadership potential.

4. **Evaluation must balance helping the principal grow with holding the principal accountable.** Unless a focus on growth is inextricably tied to accountability, neither approach tends to work well. Helping principals to grow without accountability can easily become merely advice; accountability without a focus on growth

is pointless. Further, within a legal framework, in order for evaluation to be used for personnel decisions (i.e., accountability), in most instances, opportunities for growth must be provided as well.

5. **Communication.** The evaluation system should be informed by principals and other stakeholders and be adapted over time to reflect new understandings of what they contribute to student achievement. To achieve this worthy goal, it is imperative that evaluators provide thoughtful, clear, and practical guidance for quality work, and that principals communicate with evaluators about their own growth and efforts. Simply stated: communicate early, communicate often, and communicate effectively.

Tools for Principal Improvement

Many resources are needed to help principals grow professionally. Sometimes, principals need support developing or simply meeting their performance standards; other times, they need help supporting, enhancing, and sustaining high-quality performance. It is incumbent upon both principal evaluators and principals themselves to focus on systematic growth in their quest for improvement. I recommend two tools in particular that the evaluator can use to support principal improvement: the Support Dialogue and the Performance Improvement Plan.

The Support Dialogue is a district-level discussion between the evaluator and the principal. It is an optional process to promote conversation about performance in order to address specific needs or desired areas for professional growth. The Support Dialogue process should not be construed as applying only to poorly performing principals; it is an option that is open to any principal who desires assistance in a particular area. The entire Support Dialogue process is intended to be completed in a relatively short time period (e.g., within six weeks) as it offers targeted support.

During the initial conference, both the evaluator and the principal share what each will do to support the principal's growth (see sample prompts in Figure 6.1) and decide when to meet again. To facilitate the improvements, they may choose to fill out the optional Support Dialogue Form (Figure 6.2). After the agreed-upon time to receive support and implement changes in professional practice has elapsed, the evaluator and principal meet again to discuss the effect of the changes (see sample follow-up prompts in Figure 6.1).

FIGURE 6.1

Sample Prompts in Support Dialogue

Sample Prompts for the Initial Conversation

What challenges have you encountered in addressing _____ (tell specific concern)?

What have you tried to address the concern of _____ (tell specific concern)?

What support can I or others in the division provide you?

Sample Prompts for the Follow-Up Conversation

Last time we met, we talked about _____ (tell specific concern). What has gone well? What has not gone as well?

FIGURE 6.2

Sample Support Dialogue Form (Optional)

Directions: Principals and evaluators may use this form to facilitate discussion on areas that need additional support.

What is the area of targeted support?

_____

_____

_____

_____

What are some of the issues in the area that are causing difficulty?

_____

_____

_____

_____

What strategies have you already tried, and what was the result?

_____

_____

_____

_____

What new strategies or resources might facilitate improvement in this area?

_____

_____

_____

_____

Principal's Name: _____

Principal's Signature: _____   Date: _____

Evaluator's Name: _____

Evaluator's Signature: _____   Date: _____

The Performance Improvement Plan has a more formal structure than the Support Dialogue. It is used to notify a principal that his or her performance requires improvement. A Performance Improvement Plan is designed to help a principal address areas of concern through targeted supervision and additional resources (see Figure 6.3 for a sample form). It may be used by an evaluator at any point during the year, and may be implemented if a principal meets certain predetermined criteria for intervention established by the school district (e.g., a rating of Partially Effective on two performance standards, or Ineffective on a single performance standard).

When a principal is placed on a Performance Improvement Plan, the evaluator must

- Provide written notification to the principal of the areas of concern that need to be addressed;
- Formulate a Performance Improvement Plan in conjunction with the principal; and
- Review the results of the Performance Improvement Plan with the principal within established timelines.

Assistance may include support from a professional peer or supervisor; conferences, classes, and workshops on specific topics; or other resources to be identified.

Figure 6.4 highlights key differences between the Support Dialogue and the Performance Improvement Plan.

Frequently Asked Questions

Q: What are the particular challenges to implementing the system described in this book?

A: One of the initial challenges is time. Although it may take an initial investment of time for principals and evaluators to become accustomed to the evaluation system, this time commitment is significantly reduced once the stakeholders learn how to use it.

Another challenge is helping principals to understand the expectations placed on them by the new evaluation system. Previously, they may not have had an opportunity to provide input into their own evaluation or been required to submit artifacts as evidence of successful performance. If so, such changes will take some time to get used to. Evaluators should encourage principals to collect artifacts as the year progresses and to analyze and reflect on them as they are created, rather than waiting until the end of the year.

Q: What are the main benefits of implementing the system?

A: One of the main benefits is that a comprehensive system allows both the evaluator *and* the principal to get a full picture of the latter's performance. At the same time, the fact that the system described in this book has only seven performance standards allows evaluators to focus on the principal's major duties.

FIGURE 6.3

Sample Performance Improvement Plan Form

Principal: _____   School: _____

Evaluator: _____   School Year: _____

Performance Standard Number	Performance Deficiencies Within the Standard to Be Corrected	Resources/Assistance Provided & Activities to Be Completed by the Employee	Target Dates

The principal's signature denotes receipt of the form and acknowledgment that the evaluator has notified the employee of unacceptable performance.

Principal's Name: _____

Principal's Signature: _____   Date Initiated: _____

Evaluator's Name: _____

Evaluator's Signature: _____   Date Initiated: _____

FIGURE 6.3 (*continued*)

Sample Performance Improvement Plan Form

Results of Performance Improvement Plan

(Note: These sections are to be completed collaboratively by the evaluator and the principal. Pages may be added, if needed.)

Performance Standard Number	Performance Deficiencies Within the Standard to Be Corrected	Comments	Review Dates

Final recommendation based on outcome of Performance Improvement Plan:

☐ The performance deficiencies have been satisfactorily corrected: The principal is no longer on a *Performance Improvement Plan.*

☐ The deficiencies were not corrected. The principal is recommended for dismissal.

Principal's Name: _____

Principal's Signature: _____ Date Reviewed: _____

Signature denotes the review occurred, not necessarily agreement with the final recommendation.

Evaluator's Name: _____

Evaluator's Signature: _____ Date Reviewed: _____

FIGURE 6.4

Characteristics of a Support Dialogue
and a Performance Improvement Plan

	Support Dialogue	Performance Improvement Plan
Purpose	To aid principals who could benefit from targeted performance improvement or who would like to systematically focus on their own professional growth.	To aid principals who receive Ineffective or Partially Effective ratings in their performance evaluations.
Process Initiated By	Evaluator or principal	Evaluator
Required Documentation	Documentation required: None Support documentation may include memo or other record of the discussion and other documentation at the district level (e.g., site visit forms, analysis of student achievement data, financial audits)	Documentation required: Performance Improvement Plan; superintendent notification
Expected Outcomes	Performance improvement is documented and the Support Dialogue remains ongoing at the discretion of either the evaluator or the principal. If no performance improvement occurs, Performance Improvement Plan may be initiated.	If adequate improvement occurs, evaluator recommends continued employment of principal. If improvement does not occur or is insufficient, evaluator may recommend that principal either continue with the Performance Improvement Plan or be dismissed from employment.

Q: How does the system measure principal effectiveness?

A: The principal evaluation system I've put forward measures principal effectiveness based on research-based standards and indicators rather than on the principal's own perceptions of his or her performance. Interestingly, most effective principals don't always identify themselves as such and are often more open to continued growth than their less effective peers.

Q: Which performance standard do principals tend to find the most challenging?

A: Typically, principals find Standard 7 (Student Progress) to be the most challenging because it holds them accountable for ensuring that everything that goes on in the school is related directly to the student's success. After all, aren't principals the ones who foster and help sustain the climate in which learning occurs? Don't they set expectations for high teacher and student performance? Don't they keep the organization running smoothly and efficiently so that the focus is on learning? Perhaps most important, don't they help hire, induct, develop, and evaluate the students' teachers?

Conclusion

Principal evaluation matters because *principals matter.* The research is clear that principals contribute substantially to student success, accounting for approximately one-quarter of the total school-level variation in student achievement, after controlling for student socioeconomic background factors.[2]

If we attempt to reform education without focusing on principalship quality in the school, the effort is unlikely to succeed. To quote Pont, Nusche, and Moorman:

> As the key intermediary between the classroom, the individual school, and the education system as a whole, effective school leadership is essential to improve the efficiency and equity of schooling. Within each individual school,

leadership can contribute to improved student learning by shaping the conditions and climate in which teaching and learning occur. Beyond the school borders, school leaders can connect and adapt schools to changing external environments. And at the school-systems interface, school leadership provides a bridge between internal school improvement processes and externally initiated reform.[3]

I am fully convinced that educational reform doesn't happen in the statehouse or the White House; it happens in the schoolhouse. When principals get better, schools get better. Indeed, there is no other formula for school improvement. Why? Because principals matter extraordinarily.

Notes

1. Joint Committee on Standards for Educational Evaluation, 2009.
2. Louis, Leithwood, Wahlstrom, & Anderson, 2010.
3. Pont, Nusche, & Moorman, 2008, p. 16.

Part 2

Comprehensive Set
of Principal Performance
Standards, Indicators,
and Rubrics

Performance Standard 1: Instructional Leadership

The principal fosters the success of all students by facilitating the development, communication, implementation, and evaluation of a shared vision of teaching and learning that leads to student academic progress and school improvement.

Sample Performance Indicators

Examples may include, but are not limited to, the following:

The principal

1.1   Leads the collaborative development and sustainment of a compelling shared vision for educational improvement and works collaboratively with staff, students, parents, and other stakeholders to develop a mission and programs consistent with the district's strategic plan.

1.2   Collaboratively plans, implements, supports, monitors, and evaluates instructional programs that enhance teaching and student academic progress and lead to school improvement.

1.3   Analyzes current academic achievement data and instructional strategies to make appropriate educational decisions to improve classroom instruction, increase student achievement, and improve overall school effectiveness.

1.4   Possesses knowledge of research-based instructional best practices in the classroom.

1.5   Works collaboratively with staff to identify student needs and to design, revise, and monitor instruction to ensure effective delivery of the required curriculum.

1.6   Provides teachers with resources for the successful implementation of effective instructional strategies.

1.7   Monitors and evaluates the use of diagnostic, formative, and summative assessment to provide timely and accurate feedback to students and parents, and to inform instructional practices.

1.8   Provides collaborative leadership for the design and implementation of effective and efficient schedules that protect and maximize instructional time.

1.9   Provides the focus for continued learning of all members of the school community.

1.10   Supports professional development and instructional practices that incorporate the use of achievement data and result in increased student progress.

1.11   Participates in professional development alongside teachers when instructional strategies are being taught for future implementation.

1.12   Demonstrates the importance of professional development by providing adequate time and resources for teachers and staff to participate in professional learning (i.e., peer observation, mentoring, coaching, study groups, learning teams).

1.13   Evaluates the impact professional development has on the staff/school improvement and student academic progress.

Highly Effective	Effective *(Expected level of performance)*	Partially Effective	Ineffective
In addition to meeting the requirements for Effective, the principal actively and consistently employs innovative and effective leadership strategies that maximize student academic progress and result in a shared vision of teaching and learning that reflects excellence.	The principal fosters the success of all students by facilitating the development, communication, implementation, and evaluation of a shared vision of teaching and learning that leads to student academic progress and school improvement.	The principal inconsistently fosters the success of students by facilitating the development, communication, implementation, or evaluation of a shared vision of teaching and learning that leads to student academic progress and school improvement.	The principal does not foster the success of all students by facilitating the development, communication, implementation, or evaluation of a shared vision of teaching and learning that leads to student academic progress and school improvement.

Performance Standard 2: School Climate

The principal fosters the success of all students by developing, advocating, and sustaining an academically rigorous, positive, and safe school climate for all stakeholders.

Sample Performance Indicators

Examples may include, but are not limited to, the following:

The principal

2.1   Incorporates knowledge of the social, cultural, leadership, and political dynamics of the school community to cultivate a positive academic learning environment.

2.2   Consistently models and collaboratively promotes high expectations, mutual respect, concern, and empathy for students, staff, parents, and community.

2.3   Utilizes shared decision making and collaboration to build relationships with all stakeholders and maintain positive school morale.

2.4   Models and inspires trust and a risk-tolerant environment by sharing information and power.

2.5   Maintains a collegial environment and supports the staff through the stages of the change process.

2.6   Addresses barriers to teacher and staff performance and provides positive working conditions to encourage retention of highly effective personnel.

2.7   Develops and/or implements a Safe School plan that manages crisis situations in an effective and timely manner.

2.8   Involves students, staff, parents, and the community to create and sustain a positive, safe, and healthy learning environment that reflects state, district, and local school rules, policies, and procedures.

2.9   Develops and/or implements best practices in schoolwide behavior management that are effective within the school community and communicates behavior management expectations to students, teachers, and parents.

2.10 Is visible and approachable, and dedicates time to listen to the concerns of students, teachers, and other stakeholders.

2.11 Maintains a positive, inviting school environment that promotes and assists in the development of the whole child/student and values every child/student as an important member of the school community.

Highly Effective	Effective (Expected level of performance)	Partially Effective	Ineffective
In addition to meeting the requirements for Effective, the principal seeks out new opportunities or substantially improves existing programs to create an environment where students and stakeholders thrive and the rigor of academic expectations has significantly increased as evident through results.	The principal fosters the success of all students by developing, advocating, and sustaining an academically rigorous, positive, and safe school climate for all stakeholders.	The principal inconsistently promotes the success of all students by developing, advocating, or sustaining an academically rigorous, positive, or safe school climate for all stakeholders.	The principal does not promote the success of all students by developing, advocating, or sustaining an academically rigorous, positive, or safe school climate for all stakeholders.

Performance Standard 3: Human Resources Leadership

The principal fosters effective human resources leadership by assisting with selection and induction, and by supporting, evaluating, and retaining quality instructional and support personnel.

Sample Performance Indicators

Examples may include, but are not limited to, the following:

The principal

3.1   Actively participates in the selection process, where applicable, and assigns highly effective staff in a fair and equitable manner based on school needs, assessment data, and local and state requirements.

3.2   Supports formal building-level employee induction processes and informal procedures to support and assist all new personnel.

3.3   Provides a mentoring process for all new and targeted instructional personnel, as well as cultivates leadership potential through personal mentoring.

3.4   Manages the supervision and evaluation of staff in accordance with local and state requirements.

3.5   Properly implements the teacher and staff evaluation systems, supports the important role evaluation plays in teacher and staff development, and evaluates performance of personnel using multiple sources.

3.6   Documents deficiencies and proficiencies, provides timely formal and informal feedback on strengths and weaknesses, and provides support, resources, and remediation for teachers and staff to improve job performance.

3.7   Makes appropriate recommendations relative to personnel transfer, retention, promotion, and dismissal consistent with established policies and procedures and with student academic progress as a primary consideration.

3.8   Recognizes and supports the achievements of highly effective teachers and staff and provides them opportunities for increased responsibility.

3.9   Maximizes human resources by building on the strengths of teachers and staff members and providing them with professional development opportunities to grow professionally and gain self-confidence in their skills.

Highly Effective	Effective (Expected level of performance)	Partially Effective	Ineffective
In addition to meeting the requirements for Effective, the principal consistently demonstrates expertise in human resources leadership, which results in a highly productive workforce (e.g., highly satisfied stakeholders, increased student learning, teacher leaders).	The principal fosters effective human resources leadership by assisting with selection and induction, and by supporting, evaluating, and retaining quality instructional and support personnel.	The principal inconsistently assists with selection and induction, or inconsistently supports, evaluates, and retains quality instructional and support personnel.	The principal inadequately assists with selection and induction, or inadequately supports, evaluates, and retains quality instructional and support personnel.

Performance Standard 4: Organizational Management

The principal fosters the success of all students by supporting, managing, and overseeing the school's organization, operation, and use of resources.

Sample Performance Indicators

Examples may include, but are not limited to, the following:

The principal

4.1   Demonstrates and communicates a working knowledge and understanding of the state's public education rules, regulations, and laws, and school district policies and procedures.

4.2   Establishes and enforces rules and policies to ensure a safe, secure, efficient, and orderly facility and grounds.

4.3   Monitors and provides supervision efficiently for the physical plant and all related activities through an appropriately prioritized process.

4.4   Identifies potential organizational, operational, or resource-related problems and deals with them in a timely, consistent, and effective manner.

4.5   Establishes and uses accepted procedures to develop short- and long-term goals through effective allocation of resources.

4.6   Reviews fiscal records regularly to ensure accountability for all funds.

4.7   Plans and prepares a fiscally responsible budget to support the school's mission and goals.

4.8   Follows state and local policies with regard to finances and school accountability and reporting.

4.9   Implements strategies for the inclusion of staff and stakeholders in various planning processes, shares in management decisions, and delegates duties as applicable, resulting in a smoothly operating workplace.

Highly Effective	Effective (Expected level of performance)	Partially Effective	Ineffective
In addition to meeting the requirements for Effective, the principal is exemplary at organizational management, demonstrating proactive decision making, coordinating efficient operations, and maximizing available resources.	The principal fosters the success of all students by supporting, managing, and overseeing the school's organization, operation, and use of resources.	The principal inconsistently supports, manages, or oversees the school's organization, operation, and use of resources.	The principal inadequately supports, manages, or oversees the school's organization, operation, and use of resources.

Performance Standard 5: Communication and Community Relations

The principal fosters the success of all students by communicating and collaborating effectively with stakeholders.

Sample Performance Indicators

Examples may include, but are not limited to, the following:

The principal

5.1   Plans for and solicits staff, parent, and stakeholder input to promote effective decision making and communication when appropriate.

5.2   Communicates long- and short-term goals and the school improvement plan to all stakeholders.

5.3   Disseminates information to staff, parents, and other stakeholders in a timely manner through multiple channels and sources.

5.4   Involves students, parents, staff, and other stakeholders in a collaborative effort to establish positive relationships.

5.5   Maintains visibility and accessibility to students, parents, staff, and other stakeholders.

5.6   Speaks and writes in an explicit and professional manner to students, parents, staff, and other stakeholders.

5.7   Provides a variety of opportunities for parent and family involvement in school activities.

5.8   Collaborates and networks with colleagues and stakeholders to effectively utilize the resources and expertise available in the local community.

5.9   Advocates for students and acts to influence local, district, and state decisions affecting student learning.

5.10   Assesses, plans for, responds to, and interacts with the larger political, social, economic, legal, and cultural context that affects schooling based on relevant evidence.

Highly Effective	Effective *(Expected level of performance)*	Partially Effective	Ineffective
In addition to meeting the requirements for Effective, the principal proactively seeks and creates innovative and productive methods to communicate and engage effectively with stakeholders.	The principal fosters the success of all students by communicating and collaborating effectively with stakeholders.	The principal inconsistently communicates or infrequently collaborates on issues of importance to stakeholders.	The principal demonstrates inadequate or detrimental communication or collaboration with stakeholders.

Performance Standard 6: Professionalism

The principal fosters the success of all students by demonstrating professional standards and ethics, engaging in continuous professional development, and contributing to the profession.

Sample Performance Indicators

Examples may include, but are not limited to, the following:

The principal

6.1 Creates a culture of respect, understanding, sensitivity, and appreciation for students, staff, and other stakeholders, and models these attributes on a daily basis.

6.2 Works within professional and ethical guidelines to improve student learning and to meet school, district, and state requirements.

6.3 Maintains a professional appearance and demeanor.

6.4 Models professional behavior and cultural competency to students, staff, and other stakeholders.

6.5 Maintains confidentiality.

6.6 Maintains a positive and forthright attitude.

6.7 Provides leadership in sharing ideas and information with staff and other professionals.

6.8 Works in a collegial and collaborative manner with other administrators, school personnel, and other stakeholders to promote and support the vision, mission, and goals of the school district.

6.9 Assumes responsibility for own professional development by contributing to and supporting the development of the profession through service as an instructor, mentor, coach, presenter, and/or researcher.

6.10 Remains current with research related to educational issues, trends, and practices and maintains a high level of technical and professional knowledge.

Highly Effective	Effective *(Expected level of performance)*	Partially Effective	Ineffective
In addition to meeting the requirements for Effective, the principal demonstrates professionalism beyond the school district through published works, formal presentation(s), and/or formal recognition(s) or award(s).	The principal fosters the success of students by demonstrating professional standards and ethics, engaging in continuous professional development, and contributing to the profession.	The principal is inconsistent in demonstrating professional standards, engaging in continuous professional development, or in contributing to the profession.	The principal shows disregard for professional standards and ethics, engaging in continuous professional development, or contributing to the profession.

Performance Standard 7: Student Progress

The principal's leadership results in acceptable, measurable student academic progress based on established standards.

Sample Performance Indicators

Examples may include, but are not limited to, the following:

The principal

7.1   Collaboratively develops, implements, and monitors the school improvement plan that results in increased student academic progress.

7.2   Utilizes research-based techniques for gathering and analyzing data from multiple measures to use in making decisions related to student academic progress and school improvement.

7.3   Communicates assessment results to multiple internal and external stakeholders.

7.4   Collaborates with teachers and staff to monitor and improve multiple measures of student progress through the analysis of data, the application of educational research, and the implementation of appropriate intervention and enrichment strategies.

7.5   Utilizes faculty meetings, team/department meetings, and professional development activities to focus on student progress outcomes.

7.6   Provides evidence that students are meeting measurable, reasonable, and appropriate achievement goals.

7.7   Demonstrates responsibility for school academic achievement through proactive interactions with faculty/staff, students, and other stakeholders.

7.8   Collaboratively develops, implements, and monitors long- and short-range achievement goals that address varied student populations according to state guidelines.

7.9   Ensures that teachers' student achievement goals are aligned with building-level goals for increased student academic progress and for meeting state benchmarks.

7.10 Sets benchmarks and implements appropriate strategies and interventions to accomplish desired outcomes.

Highly Effective	Effective *(Expected level of performance)*	Partially Effective	Ineffective
In addition to meeting the requirements for Effective, the principal's leadership results in a high level of student academic progress with all populations of learners.	The principal's leadership results in acceptable, measurable student academic progress based on established standards.	The principal's leadership results in student academic progress that inconsistently meets the established standards.	The principal's leadership consistently results in inadequate student academic progress.

Part 3

Principal
Evaluation Tools
You Can Use

Steps for Implementing a Principal Evaluation System

The guidelines presented in this section are intended to assist school officials with the process of moving from the concept of a principal evaluation system to its actual design and implementation. Although the specific steps may vary from organization to organization, the ones recommended here have been extensively field-tested and found to produce effective performance evaluation systems through a relatively efficient development process.

Step 1: Taking Stock

This step requires taking stock of school and district goals. To better determine a district's goals (both formal and informal), it is important to review documents, meet with stakeholders, and learn more about community expectations specifically related to performance evaluation.

Activity: **Acquire and extend understanding of participants and their schools' evaluation needs.**

- Appoint and meet with members of an evaluation design team or steering committee.
- Meet with representatives of various stakeholder groups.
- Review documents developed to date related to organizational strategic plans, identified evaluation needs, and existing evaluation systems.

Activity: **Analyze existing evaluation systems.**

- Conduct SWOT analysis: Identify the strengths and weaknesses of the current evaluation system, as well as opportunities for and threats to the development of a new one.
- Solicit input from instructional staff and administration.
- Determine which components and processes (if any) of the existing evaluation system will be incorporated into the new one.
- Determine the necessary criteria for development of a successful new evaluation system (e.g., decision rules for the evaluation committee, necessary elements for evaluation).

Step 2: Building a Foundation

Once there is a clear understanding of the schools' overall goals and the context for evaluation, districtwide program goals must be translated into position expectations based on a common set of assumptions about the role of evaluation, the legal requirements of a viable evaluation system, agreement on a basic evaluation model, and ability to judge the evaluation system's integrity. This step builds a research-based and legally sound foundation for the evaluation development process that is to follow.

Activity: **Determine the purposes of the evaluation system.**

- Solicit input on the district's desired direction so that the evaluation system can remain viable for the foreseeable future.
- Analyze the primary purpose of the new system— professional growth (formative individual objective), accountability (summative organizational objective), or a balance between the two.

Activity: **Select an evaluation model to guide development of the evaluation system.**

- Consider the key features of evaluation models under consideration.
- Adopt or adapt the model.

Activity: **Analyze the Joint Committee Personnel Evaluation Standards for development of a sound evaluation system.**

- Review the standards: *propriety, utility, feasibility,* and *accuracy (validity).*
- Consider the implications of adopting the standards on specific components of the evaluation system.

Step 3: Developing a Framework for Defining Job Expectations

Once a solid foundation for developing the new evaluation system is in place, the more tangible work of defining job expectations can begin. Materials developed reflecting competencies and performance standards should be reviewed for reference and integration into recommended roles and responsibilities. Reference materials from other school districts, international schools, professional associations, and so on should be reviewed for consideration in the development process. Principals should craft the content and language of the roles and responsibilities during the development process with technical assistance and facilitation provided as needed.

Activity: **Analyze documents related to principals' roles and responsibilities.**

- Review principal job descriptions and required competencies.
- Review performance standards.

Activity: **Review the research related to principals' roles and responsibilities.**

- Review current research regarding qualities of effective principals.
- Review current research on principal evaluation.
- Review any applicable state or local statutes, rules, or regulations related to principal evaluation.

Activity: **Develop drafts of principal performance standards.**

- Review samples of possible performance standards.
- Develop draft versions of principal performance standards.
- Refine final versions of principal performance standards.

Step 4: Developing Implementation Procedures

Once the performance standards are established, the nuts and bolts of implementation can be decided. Questions that need to be addressed include the following:

- What data sources can be used to collect evidence of a principal's performance for each of the standards?
- What are the procedures and timelines for collecting data from each source?
- How will principal performance be rated?
- What will be the procedures for handling principals who receive unacceptable ratings?

Activity: **Define methods for collecting data about principal performance.**

- Consider available methods for collecting performance data. Options may include the following:
  - Formal and informal observations
  - Student surveys
  - Documentation logs and portfolios
  - Principal self-reflection
  - Measures of student progress
- Select data-collection methods to be incorporated in the new evaluation system.
- Develop procedures for using each data-collection method.
- Resolve issues related to combining data drawn from multiple sources.

Activity: **Develop guidelines for rating performance.**

- Develop a rating scale for use with summative evaluation.
- Review and revise the rating scale, paying special attention to terminology.
- Develop a performance appraisal rubric that defines different levels of performance.
- Review and revise a behavioral summary scale.

Activity: **Develop instruments for recording performance information.**

- Identify types of assessment forms to be used (e.g., observation protocols, portfolio guidelines, client surveys, summative evaluation forms, improvement assistance plans).
- Review examples of forms for content and formatting.
- Develop draft versions of forms.
- Refine final versions of forms.

Activity: **Determine a timetable and procedures for implementation of the evaluation system.**

- Determine evaluation cycles (e.g., 1-year cycle, 3-year cycle).
- Develop a sequence of data-collection steps for principals with differing levels of experience.
- Identify a feasible timetable for data collection.
- Determine specific procedural steps for the evaluation.

Step 5: Developing Training Material for a Pilot Evaluation System

Create a performance evaluation handbook that includes the following elements:

1. Introduction
2. Explanation of the evaluation system
3. Evaluation criteria
4. Performance standards
5. Evaluation instruments
6. Implementation procedures

Step 6: Providing Comprehensive Training for Evaluators and Principals

There are two main factors that can lead to the failure of any major reform initiative, including a principal evaluation system: *flawed design* and *lack of fidelity in implementation.* If an evaluation system is flawed in its design, then no level of effort short of redesigning the system will solve the problem. However, even if the evaluation system is properly designed and includes all salient features, it still will fail without fidelity in implementation. If an evaluation system is not implemented consistently, it will become (or remain) idiosyncratic and unsystematic. To avoid flawed design, follow carefully and thoroughly the first five steps recommended here. To ensure fidelity in implementation, institute a professional development program designed to help ensure proper implementation.

Professional development is not a luxury—it is essential for successful restructuring. An evaluation project that only considers the design and development issues is only partially complete. A quality, comprehensive, and ongoing professional development program should be planned and budgeted from the beginning of the project.

Activity: **Develop an effective professional development program for both evaluators and principals that reflects current research on educational leadership and includes the following key components:**

- Participatory planning of professional development activities by stakeholders to build relevance and ownership
- Engaging activities that support learning through hands-on, active experiences
- Reality-based strategies (e.g., simulations) or real-time approaches that reinforce collegial networks and teaming
- A delivery system that includes job-embedded experiences to extend learning beyond the training site and into the workplace
- Training sessions that use a variety of approaches such as demonstration, monitored practice and feedback, technology, study groups, and collegial problem solving
- If taking a "train-the-trainer" approach, cadres of trainers to serve member schools with teams working from the bottom up to identify and implement training components

- Ongoing professional development activities that are cumulative and sustained over the implementation period

Activity: **Enhance trainers' understanding of the new evaluation system by familiarizing them with the major components in the evaluation handbook developed in Step 5.**

Activity: **Provide activities for evaluator and principal skill development, including the following elements:**

- Evaluation orientation (i.e., how the new evaluation system works)
- An overview of documentation tools (e.g., observation format, documentation log design)
- Training to ensure inter-rater reliability in conducting evaluations (must be provided for evaluators; may be provided for principals)
- Skills-based professional development in activities related to evaluation (e.g., how to develop a document log, how to design and set appropriate goals)

Step 7: Piloting and Implementing the New Evaluation System

A broad-based pilot program will offer opportunities to tailor the new evaluation system to the needs of the school or district; offer the opportunity to monitor the feasibility, utility, accuracy, and propriety of the system; and ensure that the system is fair to all users as well as conceptually, technically, and legally sound.

Here are the steps necessary for a successful pilot program:

1. Develop a plan for implementation of a full pilot program based on feedback from school and district staff.
2. Provide training for evaluators and principals in the pilot program.
3. Monitor implementation of the system during the pilot program and gather evidence of its viability (e.g., What works? What doesn't?).
4. Reconvene the original evaluation design team or steering committee to review results near the conclusion of the pilot program (usually the end of one academic year).
5. Revise the system and implement it districtwide.

How the Characteristics of Teacher Evaluation Systems Can Inform Principal Evaluation

Because most extant research regarding standards-based evaluation systems in education is focused on teacher evaluation, it makes sense to offer an overview of the key features of teacher evaluation systems that can also inform the design and implementation of principal evaluation systems. The following bulleted items are findings or implications drawn from extant research studies that examined standards-based teacher evaluation systems. If you are interested in further exploring the research base, the specific studies are included in the resources list at the end of Part 3.

- Standards-based teacher evaluation has at its core a vision of teaching elaborated with a broad conception of the profession, comprehensive standards, and detailed criteria through rubrics. The standards are derived from research and theory on instruction and are intended to be public and consensus-based and to provide explicit performance expectations.
- All standards-based models use rubrics to rate teacher performance as defined by a behaviorally anchored rating scale that describes the performance expected at each level. Examples of performance levels include the following:
  - Distinguished, Superior, Proficient, Needs Improvement, Unacceptable

- Highly Effective, Effective, Partially Effective, Ineffective (these are the levels used in the evaluation system recommended in this book)
- Distinguished, Proficient, Basic, Unsatisfactory
- Exemplary, Proficient, Unsatisfactory
- Advanced, Proficient, Conditional

- Standards-based teacher evaluation models capture an especially rich picture of the educator's performance by using multiple measures (e.g. client surveys, portfolios, written reflection). Some models include student performance as a measure of teacher effectiveness.
- In most standards-based teacher evaluation systems, the building administrator functions as the teacher evaluator. Ideally, however, the evaluation would be conducted both by the building administrator and by subject-area or grade-level specialists who receive extensive training to ensure inter-rater reliability. (Principal evaluation systems almost always include a district-level administrator [e.g., superintendent, assistant superintendent] as the evaluator.)

Strengths of Standards-Based Evaluation Systems

Standards-based evaluation systems for both teachers and principals

- Have adequate external validity, as demonstrated by the fact that teachers who receive positive evaluations have been found to help their students make higher achievement gains;
- Are credible as methods for measuring the quality of teachers' and principals' work;
- Can facilitate decisions related to performance pay, serving as a foundation for compensation plans based on knowledge, skills, and outcomes;
- Can be more effective than traditional evaluation models in identifying incompetent teachers or principals and facilitating their dismissal; and
- Are valuable regardless of the degree to which they predict student achievement or identify ineffective staff in that they support self-improvement efforts on the part of teachers and principals and contribute to an overall atmosphere of professionalism.

Here are some findings regarding the strengths of standards-based evaluation systems focused on teachers that educators would do well to consider when creating a system focused on principals:

- Teachers suggest that standards-based evaluation systems contribute to a common dialogue about quality instruction that can be used to improve their practice.

- Teachers perceive standards-based evaluation systems as providing more comprehensive, specific, and clear expectations for performance than other evaluation systems in which they'd participated, and respond positively to the opportunity to provide input into the process.
- Teachers tend to accept the standards, procedures, and outcomes of standards-based evaluation systems, agreeing that such systems both increase teacher accountability and help teachers improve professionally.
- When teachers find standards to be understandable and relevant to good teaching, they also perceive the feedback they receive to be effective and helpful.
- Most teachers accept performance standards as consistent with their view of good teaching and consistent with their school's philosophy.
- Teachers report that a standards-based evaluation process can lead to more reflection, to better alignment between their teaching and student standards, greater organization, improved lesson planning, and heightened classroom management skills.
- Performance-based teacher evaluation systems have been found to have a substantial degree of criterion validity, in some cases comparable to evaluation systems in the private sector and much higher than commonly found in education.
- Students of teachers with higher scores on standards-based evaluations produce greater learning gains than predicted based on the students' prior achievement

and their students' demographic characteristics than do teachers with lower scores.

- Teachers' dispositions toward standards-based teacher evaluation systems depend on a variety of factors, including school level—high school teachers perceive the systems less favorably than do their elementary peers—and how well principals manage and use the evaluation process.

Weaknesses of Standards-Based Evaluation Systems

Potential weaknesses of standards-based evaluation systems for both teachers and principals include the following:

- They can lead to an increase in paperwork and time spent engaging with evaluators, which can lead to burdensome time constraints.
- Principals or teachers may find the distinctions among performance levels unclear, especially between "proficient" and "distinguished." Some urban teachers feel that performance-level expectations for the highest levels are unrealistic in their school districts.
- Feedback can be too summative and not adequately formative, especially when it's more focused on performance levels and scores rather than on in-depth discussion of strengths and weaknesses and plans for improvement.
- Implementation of the system can be disorganized and confusing, especially if many changes are being made throughout the year.
- Principals and teachers may have concerns about the fairness of the process.
- The workload involved in preparing portfolios may be onerous, and those being evaluated may be unclear as to expected content and timelines.
- Feedback may be lacking, particularly as regards in-depth discussions on the results of evaluations and suggestions on how to improve performance.

Here are some findings regarding the weaknesses of standards-based evaluation systems focused on teachers that educators would do well to consider when creating a system focused on principals:

- Teacher perceptions of the nature, quality, and acceptability of feedback vary depending on the qualifications of evaluators and on teachers' relationships with them.
- In some cases, evaluators' lack of sufficient subject content knowledge and content-specific teaching strategies limit the depth and credibility of the feedback they provide.
- Standards-based evaluation systems are more likely to lead to changes in instructional processes, such as classroom management and interactions with students and record keeping, than changes in subject content or content-specific instructional strategies.
- Administrators share that standards-based evaluation systems require them to conduct more frequent classroom observations and related conferences (particularly for pretenured teachers), gather more extensive evidence, and write more detailed evaluation reports than they otherwise would.
- Evaluators can be inconsistent in terms of the processes they use and the scores they assign, and their feedback can lack specificity and timeliness.
- Some teachers find that standards do not apply to their subjects (e.g., special education, music, art).
- Though teachers rated as "distinguished" tended to have positive gains in their practice, those rated

"proficient" or "basic" did not, raising concerns that the system did not adequately discriminate between "proficient" and "basic" levels.

- Teachers who demonstrate proficiency while being observed may not practice it in their daily, routine teaching.

Suggested Resources

If you'd like to learn more about standards-based evaluation practices, consider the following publications.

Conley, S., Muncy, D. E., & You, S. (2005). Standards-based evaluation and teacher career satisfaction: A structural equation modeling analysis. *Journal of Personnel Evaluation in Education, 18*(1), 39–65.

Ellet, C. D., & Teddlie, C. (2003). Teacher evaluation, teacher effectiveness, and school effectiveness: Perspectives from the USA. *Journal of Personnel Evaluation in Education, 17*(1), 101–128.

Gallagher, H. A. (2004). Vaughn Elementary's innovative teacher evaluation system: Are teacher evaluation scores related to growth in student achievement? *Peabody Journal of Education, 79*(4), 79–107.

Heneman, H. G., III., & Milanowski, A. T. (2003). Continuing assessment of teacher reaction to a standards-based teacher evaluation system. *Journal of Personnel Evaluation in Education, 17*(2), 173–195.

Holtzapple, E. (2003). Criterion-related validity evidence for a standards-based teacher evaluation system. *Journal of Personnel Evaluation in Education, 17*(3), 207–219.

Joint Committee on Standards for Educational Evaluation. (2009). *The personnel evaluation standards: How to assess personnel evaluations and personnel evaluation systems* (2nd ed.). Thousand Oaks, CA: Corwin Press.

Kimball, S. M. (2002). Analysis of feedback, enabling conditions and fairness perceptions of teachers in three school districts with new standards-based evaluation systems. *Journal of Personnel Evaluation in Education, 16*(4), 241–268.

Kyriakides, L., & Demetriou, D. (2007). Introducing a teacher evaluation system based on teacher effectiveness research: An investigation of stakeholders' perceptions. *Journal of Personnel Evaluation in Education, 20*, 43–64.

Milanowski, A. T., & Heneman, H. G., III. (2001). Assessment of teacher reactions to a standards-based evaluation system: A pilot study. *Journal of Personnel Evaluation in Education, 15*(3), 193–212.

Odden, A. (2004). Lessons learned about standards-based teacher evaluation systems. *Peabody Journal of Education, 79*(4), 126–137.

Stronge, J. H. (Ed.) (1997). *Evaluating teaching: A guide to current thinking and best practice.* Thousand Oaks, CA: Corwin Press.

Stronge, J. H. (Ed.) (2006). *Evaluating teaching: A guide to current thinking and best practice* (2nd ed.). Thousand Oaks, CA: Corwin Press.

Stronge, J. H. (2007). *Qualities of effective teachers* (2nd ed.). Alexandria, VA: ASCD.

Stronge, J. H., Richard, H. B., & Catano, N. (2008). *Qualities of effective principals.* Alexandria, VA: ASCD.

Stronge, J. H. (2010). *Evaluating what good teachers do: Eight research-based standards for assessing teacher excellence.* Larchmont, NY: Eye On Education.

Toch, T., & Rothman, R. (2008). *Rush to judgment: Teacher evaluation in public education.* Washington, DC: Education Sector.

References

American Association for Employment in Education. (2000). *Educator supply and demand in the United States.* Columbus, OH: Author.

Bamburg, J. D., & Andrews, R. L. (1991). School goals, principals, and achievement. *School Effectiveness and School Improvement, 2,* 175–191.

Barth, R. S. (1985). The leader as learner. *Educational Leadership, 42*(6), 92–94.

Barth, R. S. (2002). The culture builder. *Educational Leadership, 59*(8), 6–11.

Beck, L. G., & Murphy, J. (1994). *Ethics in educational leadership programs: An expanding role.* Thousand Oaks, CA: Corwin Press.

Beteille, T., Kalogrides, D., & Loeb, S. (2009). *Effective schools: Managing the recruitment, development, and retention of high-quality teachers* [working paper]. National Center for Analysis of Longitudinal Data in Education Research.

Blase, J., & Blase, J. (1999). *Leadership for staff development: Supporting the lifelong study of teaching and learning* (pp. 2–18). Washington, DC: Educational Resources Information Center, U.S. Department of Education.

Boreen, J., Johnson, M. K., Niday, D., & Potts, J. (2000). *Mentoring beginning teachers: Guiding, reflecting, coaching.* York, ME: Stenhouse Publishers.

Boris-Schacter, S., & Merrifield, S. (2000). Why particularly good principals don't quit. *Journal of School Leadership, 10*(1), 84–98.

Brewer, D. J. (1993). Principals and student outcomes: Evidence from U.S. high schools. *Economics of Education Review, 12*(4), 281–292.

Bridgeland, J. M., DiIulio, J. J., Streeter, R. T., Mason, J. R., & Civic, E. (2008). *One dream, two realities: Perspectives of parents on America's high schools,* Washington, DC: Civic Enterprises.

Bryk, A. S. (2010). Organizing schools for improvement. *Phi Delta Kappan, 91*(7), 23–30.

Bryk, A. S., & Schneider, B. (2002). *Trust in schools: A core resource for school improvement.* New York: Russell Sage Foundation.

Buck, F. (2007). Saving time and paper with basic technology. *Principal, 86*(30), 18–21.

Carr, N. (2011). How schools can get better media coverage in the digital news ecosystem. *eSchool News, 14*(5), 35.

Catano, N. (2002). *Content analysis of principal job descriptions and principal evaluation instruments of K–12 public education in Virginia.* Doctoral dissertation, The College of William and Mary, Williamsburg, VA.

Catano, N., & Stronge, J. H. (2006). What are principals expected to do? Congruence between principal evaluation and performance standards. *NASSP Bulletin, 90*(3), 221–237.

Cawelti, G. (1999). *Portraits of six benchmark schools: Diverse approach to improving student achievement.* Arlington, VA: Educational Research Service.

Cheney, S. (2001). *Keeping competitive: A report of a survey of 1,800 employees.* Washington, DC: Center for Workplace Preparation.

Cheng, Y. C. (1994). Principal's leadership as a critical factor for school performance: Evidence from multi-levels of primary schools. *School Effectiveness and School Improvement, 5*(3), 299–317.

Chew, J., & Andrews, D. (2010). Enabling teachers to become pedagogical leaders: Case studies of two IDEAS schools in Singapore and Australia. *Educational Research for Policy & Practice, 9*(1), 59–74.

Clifford, M., Behrstock-Sherratt, E., & Fetters, J. (2012). *The ripple effect: A synthesis of research on principal influence to inform performance evaluation design.* Washington, DC: American Institute for Research.

Cotton, K. (2003). *Principals and student achievement: What the research says.* Alexandria, VA: ASCD.

Cotton, K., & Wikelund, K. R. (1989). *Parent involvement in education.* Washington, DC: Office of Educational Research and Improvement, U.S. Department of Education.

Daly, A. J. (2009). Rigid response in an age of accountability: The potential of leadership and trust. *Educational Administration Quarterly, 45*(2), 168–216.

Danielson, C. (2001). New trends in teacher evaluation. *Educational Leadership, 58*(5), 12–16.

Danielson, C. (2002). *Enhancing student achievement: A framework for school improvement.* Alexandria, VA: ASCD.

DePasquale, F. (2012). *Principal leadership behavior and faculty trust: Is there a connection?* Pittsburgh, PA: Rosedog Books.

Drago-Severson, E. (2004). *Helping teachers learn: Principal leadership for adult growth and development.* Thousand Oaks, CA: Corwin Press.

Duke, D. L. (1997). Seeking a centrist position to counter the politics of polarization. *Phi Delta Kappan, 78*, 120–123.

Ellett, C. D., & Teddlie, C. (2003). Teacher evaluation, teacher effectiveness and school effectiveness: Perspectives from the USA. *Journal of Personnel Evaluation in Education 17*(1), 101–128.

Fink, E., & Resnick, L. B. (2001). Developing principals as instructional leaders. *Phi Delta Kappan, 82*(8), 598–606.

Friend, M. (2007, February). The coteaching partnership. *Educational Leadership, 64*(5), 48–52.

Fullan, M. (2001). *Leading in a culture of change.* San Francisco, CA: Jossey Bass.

Fullan, M. (2002, May). Principals as leaders in a culture of change. *Educational Leadership, 59*(8), 16–21.

Fullan, M., Bertani, A., & Quinn, J. (2004, April). New lessons for districtwide reform: Effective leadership for change has 10 crucial components. *Educational Leadership, 61*(7), 41–46.

Gehrke, N. (1991, April). Developing teacher leadership skills. *Eric Digest.* (ERIC Document Reproduction Service No. ED 330 691)

Goe, L., Bell, C., & Little, O. (2008). *Approaches to evaluating teacher effectiveness: A research synthesis.* Washington, DC: National Comprehensive Center for Teacher Quality.

Goldring, E., Cravens, X. C., Murphy, J., Porter, A. C., Elliott, S. N., & Carson, B. (2009). The evaluation of principals: What and how do states and urban districts assess leadership? *Elementary School Journal, 110*(1), 19–39.

Griffith, J. (2004). Relation of principal transformational leadership to school staff job satisfaction, staff turnover, and school performance. *Journal of Educational Administration, 42*(3), 333–356.

Grissom, J. A. (2011). Can good principals keep teachers in disadvantaged schools? Linking principal effectiveness to teacher satisfaction and turnover in hard-to-staff environments. *Teacher College Record, 113*(11), 2552–2585.

Grissom, J. A., & Loeb, S. (2011). Triangulating principal effectiveness: How perspectives of parents, teachers, and assistant principals identify the central importance of managerial skills. *American Educational Research Journal, 48*(5), 1091–1123.

Hallinger, P. (2005). Instructional leadership and the school principal: A passing fancy that refuses to fade away. *Leadership and Policy in School, 4,* 1–20.

Hallinger, P., Bickman, L., & Davis, K. (1996). School context, principal leadership, and student reading achievement. *Elementary School Journal, 96*(5), 527–549.

Hallinger, P., & Heck. R. H. (1996, February). Reassessing the principal's role in school effectiveness: A review of empirical research. *Educational Administration Quarterly, 32*(1), 5–44.

Hallinger, P., & Heck, R. H. (2010). Leadership for learning: Does collaborative leadership make a difference in school improvement? *Educational Management Administration & Leadership, 38*(6), 654–678.

Hands, C. (2010). Why collaborate? The differing reasons for secondary school educators' establishment of school-community partnerships. *School Effectiveness & School Improvement, 21*(2), 189–207.

Hargreaves, A., & Fink, D. (2003). Sustaining leadership. *Phi Delta Kappan, 84*(9), 693–700.

Harris, A. (2005). Leading or misleading? Distributed leadership and school improvement. *Journal of Curriculum Studies 37*(3), 255–265.

Harris, A. & Muijs, D. (2003). *Teacher leadership: A review of research.* Retrieved from http://www.teachers.org.uk/resources/pdf/t-leadership-review.pdf

Harris, S. L., & Lowery, L. (2002). A view from the classroom. *Educational Leadership, 59*(8), 64–65.

Heck, R. H., & Hallinger, P. (2009). Assessing the contribution of distributed leadership to school improvement and growth in math achievement. *American Educational Research Journal, 46*(3), 659–689.

Heck, R. H., & Marcoulides, G. A. (1996). School culture and performance: Testing the invariance of an organizational model. *School Effectiveness and School Improvement, 7*(1), 76–95.

Helm, V. M., & St. Maurice, H. (2006). Conducting a successful evaluation conference. In J. H. Stronge (Ed.), *Evaluating teaching: A guide to current thinking and best practice* (2nd ed.) (pp. 235–252). Thousand Oaks, CA: Corwin Press.

Hinchey, P. H. (2010). *Getting teacher assessment right: What policymakers can learn from research.* Boulder, CO: National Education Policy Center. Retrieved from http://nepc.colorado.edu/publication/getting-teacher-assessment-right

Hindman, J. L. (2004). The connection between qualities of effective teachers and selection interviews: The development of a teacher selection interview protocol. *Dissertation Abstracts International.* (UMI No. 3118184)

Hirsch, E. (2005). *Listening to the experts: A report on the 2004 South Carolina teacher working conditions survey.* Chapel Hill, NC: Southeast Center for Teaching Quality.

Horng, E., Klasik, D., & Loeb, S. (2010). Principal's time use and school effectiveness. *American Journal of Education, 116*(4), 491–523.

Horng, E. & Loeb, S. (2010). New thinking about instructional leadership. *Phi Delta Kappan, 92*(3), 66–69.

Howard, B. B., & McColsky, W. H. (2001). Evaluating experienced teachers. *Educational Leadership, 58*(5), 48–51.

Hoy, W. K., & Hannum, J. (1997). Middle school climate: An empirical assessment of organizational health and student achievement. *Educational Administration Quarterly, 33*(3), 290–311.

Hoy, W. K., Tarter, C. J., & Kottkamp, R. B. (1991). *Open school/healthy schools: Measuring organizational climate* [Adobe Digital Editions version].

Hoy, W. K., & Tschannen-Moran, M. (1999). Five faces of trust: An empirical confirmation in urban elementary schools. *Journal of School Leadership, 9,* 184–208.

Ingersoll, R. M. (2002). The teacher shortage: A case of wrong diagnosis and wrong prescription. *NASSP Bulletin, 86*(6), 16–31.

Ingersoll, R. M., & Kralik, J. M. (2004). *The impact of mentoring on teacher retention: What the research says.* Denver, CO: Education Commission of the States.

Ingersoll, R. M., & Strong, M. (2011). The impact of induction and mentoring programs for beginning teachers: A critical review of the research. *Review of Educational Research, 81*(2), 201–233.

Joint Committee on Standards for Educational Evaluation. (2009). *The personnel evaluation standards: How to assess personnel evaluations and personnel evaluation systems* (2nd ed.). Thousand Oaks, CA: Corwin Press.

Johnson, J. F., Jr., & Uline, C. L. (2005). Preparing educational leaders to close achievement gaps. *Theory into Practice, 44*(1), 45–52.

Kaucher, E. (2010). *Ethical decision making and effective leadership.* Ann Arbor, MI: ProQuest LLC.

Kearney, W., & Herrington, D. (2010). High-performing principals in historically low-performing minority-serving schools: A glimpse into the success of 90/90/90 Schools in South Central Texas. *National Forum of Applied Educational Research Journal, 24*(1/2), 63–72.

Kelley, R. C., Thornton, B., & Daugherty, R. (2005). Relationships between measures and school climate. *Education, 126*(1), 17–25.

Kouzes, J. M., & Posner, B. Z. (2002). *The leadership challenge* (3rd ed.). San Francisco, CA: Jossey-Bass.

Kythreotis, A., & Pashiardis, P. (1998). *The influence of school leadership styles and culture on students' achievement in Cyprus primary schools* (pp. 1–31). [Monograph]. Nicosia, Cyprus: University of Cyprus.

LaPointe, M., & Davis, S. H. (2006). Effective schools require effective principals. *Leadership, 36*(1), 16–38.

Lashway, L. (2003). *Role of the school leader.* Eugene, OR: College of Education, University of Oregon.

Leithwood, K. (2010). Characteristics of school districts that are exceptionally effective in closing the achievement gap. *Leadership & Policy in Schools, 9*(3), 245–291.

Leithwood, K., & Beatty, B. (2007). *Leading with teacher emotions in mind.* Thousand Oaks, CA: Corwin.

Leithwood, K., Harris, A., & Hopkins, D. (2008). Seven strong claims about successful school leadership. *School Leadership and Management, 28*(1), 27–42.

Leithwood, K., & Jantzi, D. (2000). Principal and teacher leadership effects: A replication. *School Leadership and Management, 20*(4), 415–434.

Leithwood, K., & Jantzi, D. (2006). Transformational school leadership for large-scale reform: Effects on students, teachers, and their classroom practices. *School Effectiveness and School Improvement, 17*(2), 201–227.

Leithwood, K., Louis, S. K., Anderson, S., & Wahlstrom, K. (2004). *How leadership influences student learning.* Learning from Research Project: University of Minnesota, Center for Applied Research and Educational Improvement (CAREI); University of Toronto, Ontario Institute for Studies in Education at the University of Toronto (OISEUT); the Wallace Foundation.

Leithwood, K., & Mascall, B. (2008). Collective leadership effects on student achievement. *Educational Administration Quarterly, 44,* 1–34.

Leithwood, K., Mascall, B., Strauss, T., Sacks, R., Memon, N., & Yashkina, A. (2007). Distributing leadership to make schools smarter: Taking the ego out of the system. *Leadership and Policy in Schools, 6*(1), 37–67.

Leithwood, K. A., & Riehl, C. (2003). *What do we already know about successful school leadership?* Washington, DC: AERA Division A Task Force on Developing Educational Leadership.

Leitner, D. (1994). Do principals affect student outcomes? *School Effectiveness and School Improvement, 5*(3), 219–238.

Lindahl, R. (2009). School climate differences between high-performing and low-performing schools that serve high-poverty populations, *NCPEA Education Leadership Review, 10*(1). Retrieved from http://cnx.org/content/m19508/latest/?collection=col10630/latest

Louis, K. S., Leithwood, K., & Wahlstrom, K. L. & Anderson, S. E. (2010). *Learning from leadership: Investigating the links to improved student learning.* Washington, DC: The Wallace Foundation.

Luekens, M. T., Lyter, D. M., & Fox, E. E. (2004). Teacher attrition and mobility: Results from the teacher follow-up survey, 2000–01. *Education Statistics Quarterly, 6*(3). Retrieved from http://nces.ed.gov/programs/quarterly/vol_6/6_3/3_5.asp

Marshak, J., & Klotz, J. (2002). *To mentor or to induct: That is the question.* Paper presented at the Annual Meeting of the Mid-South Educational Research Association, Chattanooga, Tennessee.

Marzano, R., Waters, T., & McNulty, B. A. (2005). *School leadership that works: From research to results.* Alexandria, VA: ASCD; Aurora, CO: McREL.

May, H., & Supovitz, J. A. (2011). The scope of principal efforts to improve instruction. *Educational Administration Quarterly, 47*(2), 332–352.

Mazzeo, C. (2003). *Improving teaching and learning by improving school leadership.* Washington, DC: National Governors Association Center for Best Practices.

McGrath, M. J. (2006). Dealing positively with the nonproductive teacher: A legal and ethical perspective on accountability. In J. H. Stronge (Ed.), *Evaluating teaching: A guide to current thinking and best practice* (2nd ed.) (pp. 253–267). Thousand Oaks, CA: Corwin Press.

McLaughlin, M. W. (1990). Embracing contraries: Implementing and sustaining teacher evaluation. In J. Millman and L. Darling-Hammond (Eds.), *The new handbook of teacher evaluation: Assessing elementary and secondary school teachers* (pp. 403–415). Newbury Park, CA: Sage Publications.

McLaughlin, D., & Drori, G. (2000). *School-level correlates of academic achievement: Student assessment scores in SASS public schools.* (NCES 2000-303). Washington, DC: U.S. Department of Education, National Center for Education Statistics.

Means, B. (2010). Technology and education change: Focus on student learning. *Journal of Research on Technology in Education, 42*(3), 285–307.

Mendro, R. L. (1998). Student achievement and school and teacher accountability. *Journal of Personnel Evaluation in Education, 12*(3), 257–267.

Menuey, B. P. (2005). Teachers' perceptions of professional incompetence and barriers to the dismissal process. *Journal of Personnel Evaluation in Education, 18*(4), 309–325.

Merriam-Webster Learning Dictionary. (n.d.). Retrieved from http://www.learnersdictionary.com/search/assessment

Muijs, D., & Harris, A. (2006). Teacher-led school improvement: Teacher leadership in the UK. *Teaching & Teacher Education, 22*(8), 961–972.

Mullen, C. A., & Lick, D. W. (Eds.). (1999). *New directions in mentoring: Creating a culture of synergy.* New York: Falmer Press.

Neely, E. (2005). Communicating with parents: It works both ways. *Leadership, 34*(5), 24–27.

Pajak, E., & McAfee, L. (1992). The principal as school leader, curriculum leader. *NASSP Bulletin, 7*(547), 21–29.

Painter, S. R. (2000). Principals' efficacy beliefs about teacher evaluation. *Journal of Educational Administration, 38*(4), 368–378.

Peterson, K. D. (2002). *Effective teacher hiring: A guide to getting the best.* Alexandria, VA: ASCD.

Piltch, B., & Fredericks, R. (2005, January/February). A principal's guide to school politics. *Principal, 84*(3), 10–14.

Pont, B., Nusche, D., & Moorman, H. (2008). *Improving school leadership, Volume 1: Policy and practice.* Paris: OECD.

Porterfield, K., & Carnes, M. (2010). Tools of the trade. *Principal, 89*(4), 28–30, 32, 34–35.

Portin, B., Schneider, P., DeArmond, M., & Gundlach, L. (2003, September). *Making sense of leading schools: A study of the school principalship.* Seattle, WA: Center on Reinventing Public Education.

Poston, W. K., Jr., & Manatt, R. P. (1993). Principals as evaluators: Limiting effects on school reform. *International Journal of Educational Reform, 2*(1), 41–48.

Pounder, D. G., Ogawa, R. T., & Adams, E. A. (1995). Leadership as an organization-wide phenomena: Its impact on school performance. *Educational Administration Quarterly, 31*, 564–588.

Pressley, M., Raphael, L., Gallagher, J. D., & DiBella, J. (2004). Providence–St. Mel School: How a school that works for African American students works. *Journal of Educational Psychology, 96*(2), 216–235.

Prestine, N. A., & Nelson, B. S. (2003). *How can educational leaders support and promote teaching and learning? New conceptions of learning and leading in schools.* Paper presented at the Annual Meeting of the American Educational Research Organization, Chicago, Illinois.

Quint, J. C., Akey, T. M., Rappaport, S., & Willner, C. J. (2007). *Instructional leadership, teaching quality and student achievement: Suggestive evidence from three urban school districts.* New York: Manpower Demonstration Research Corp.

Reason, C., & Reason, L. (2007). Asking the right questions. *Educational Leadership, 65*(1), 36–47.

Reeves, D. B. (2005). *Assessing educational leaders: Evaluating performance for improved individual and organizational results.* Thousand Oaks, CA: Corwin.

Reeves, D. (2006). *The learning leader.* Alexandria, VA: ASCD.

Robinson, V. J., Lloyd, C. A., & Rowe, K. J. (2008). The impact of leadership on student outcomes: An analysis of the differential effects of leadership types. *Educational Administration Quarterly, 44*(5), 635–674.

Ross, J., & Gray, P. (2006). Transformational leadership and teacher commitment to organizational values: The mediating effect of collective teacher efficacy. *School Effectiveness and School Improvement, 17*(2), 179–199.

Ruebling, C. E., Stow, S. B., Kayona, F. A., & Clarke, N. A. (2004). Instructional leadership: An essential ingredient for improving student learning. *Educational Forum, 68*, 243–252.

Sanders, W. L., & Horn, S. P. (1998). Research findings from the Tennessee value-added assessment system (TVAAS) database: Implications for educational evaluation and research. *Journal of Personnel Evaluation in Education, 12*(3), 247–256.

Sanders, W. L., & Rivers, J. C. (1996). *Cumulative and residual effects of teachers on future student academic achievement.* Knoxville, TN: University of Tennessee Value-Added Research and Assessment Center.

Shellard, E. (2005). How assessment data can improve instruction. *Principal, 84*(3), 30–32.

Shen, J., & Hsieh, C. (1999). The instructional goals of the school leadership program: Future leaders' and educational leadership professors' perspectives. *Journal of School Leadership, 9*(1), 79–91.

Silins, H., & Mulford, B. (2002). Leadership and school results. In K. Leithwood (Ed.), *The second international handbook of educational leadership and administration* (pp. 561–612). Norwell, MA: Kluwer Academic.

Smith, T. M., & Ingersoll, R. M. (2004). What are the effects of induction and mentoring on beginning teacher turnover? *American Educational Research Journal, 41*(3), 681–714. Retrieved from EBSCOhost.

Snipes, J., Doolittle, F., & Herlihy, C. (2002). *Foundations for success: Case studies of how urban school systems improve student achievement.* New York: Manpower Demonstration Research Corporation.

Stronge, J. H. (1995). Balancing individual and institutional goals in educational personnel evaluation: A conceptual framework. *Studies in Educational Evaluation, 21*(2), 131–151.

Stronge, J. H., Richard, H. B., & Catano, N. (2008). *Qualities of Effective Principals.* Alexandria, VA: ASCD.

Stronge, J. H., & Tucker, P. D. (2003). *Handbook on teacher evaluation: Assessing and improving performance.* Larchmont, NY: Eye On Education.

Supovitz, J. (2006). *The case for district-based reform: Leading, building, and sustaining school improvement.* Cambridge, MA: Harvard Education Press.

Sweeny, B. W. (2001). *Leading the teacher induction and mentoring program.* Arlington Heights, IL: Skylight Professional Development.

Togneri, W., & Anderson, S. E. (2003). *Beyond islands of excellence: What districts can do to improve instruction and achievement in all schools.* Alexandria, VA: Learning Alliance First.

Tschannen-Moran, M. (2004). *Trust matters: Leadership for successful schools.* San Francisco, CA: Jossey-Bass.

Tschannen-Moran, M. (2009). Fostering teacher professionalism in schools: The role of leadership orientation and trust. *Educational Administration Quarterly, 45*(2), 217–247.

Tschannen-Moran, M., & Hoy, W. K. (2000). A multidisciplinary analysis of the nature, meaning, and measurement of trust. *Review of Educational Research, 70*(4), 547–593.

Tucker, P. D. (1997). Lake Wobegon: Where all teachers are competent (Or, have we come to terms with the problems of incompetent teachers?). *Journal of Personnel Evaluation in Education, 11*, 103–125.

Tucker, P. D., Stronge, J. H., & Gareis, C. (2002). *Handbook on teacher portfolios for evaluation and professional development.* Larchmont, NY: Eye On Education.

United States Department of Education. (2006, Fall). *Lessons learned from school crises and emergencies.* Washington, DC: Author.

United States Department of Education. (2011). Application for new awards: Supporting effective educator development grant program. 76 *Fed. Reg.* 174. Retrieved from http://www.gpo.gov/fdsys/pkg/FR-2011-09-08/pdf/2011-23011.pdf

Usdan, M., McCloud, B., & Podmostko, M. (2000). *Leadership for student learning: Reinventing the principalship.* Washington, DC: Institute for Educational Leadership.

Wagner, T., Kegan, R., Lahey, L. L., Lemons, R. W., Garnier, J., Helsing, D., Howell, A., Rasmussen, H. T., & Vander Ark, T. (2006). *Change leadership: A practical guide to transforming our schools.* San Francisco, CA: Jossey-Bass.

Wahlstrom, K. L., & Louis, K. S. (2008). How teachers experience principal leadership: The roles of professional community, trust, efficacy, and shared responsibility. *Educational Administration Quarterly, 44*, 458–495.

Waters, T., & Grubb, S. (2004). *Leading schools: Distinguishing the essential from the important.* Retrieved from http://www.mcrel.org/PDF/Leadership OrganizationDevelopment/4005IR_LeadingSchools.pdf

Waters, J. T., Marzano, R. J., & McNulty, B. (2003). *Balanced leadership: What 30 years of research tells us about the effect of leadership on student achievement: A working paper.* Aurora, CO: McREL.

Watkins, P. (2005). The principal's role in attracting, retaining, and developing new teachers. *Clearing House, 79*(2), 83–87.

Westberg, D., Sexton, S., Mulhern, J., & Keeling, D. (2009). *The widget effect: Our national failure to acknowledge and act on differences in teacher effectiveness.* Retrieved from http://widgeteffect.org/downloads/TheWidget Effect.pdf

Witziers, B., Bosker, R. J., & Krüger, M. L. (2003). Educational leadership and student achievement: The elusive search for an association. *Educational Administration Quarterly, 39*(3), 398–425.

Wohlstetter, P., Datnow, A., & Park, P. (2008). Creating a system for data-driven decision making: Applying the principal-agent framework. *School Effectiveness and School Improvement, 19*(3), 239–259.

Wong, H. (2001, August 8). Mentoring can't do it all. *Education Week.* Retrieved from http://www.edweek.org/ew/articles/2001/08/08/43wong .h20.html

Wurtzel, J. (2007). The professional, personified: Districts find results by combining a vision of professionalism with the use of common tasks and goals. *Journal of Staff Development, 28*(4), 30–35.

Zmuda, A., Kuklis, R., & Kline, E. (2004). *Transforming schools: Creating a culture of continuous improvement.* Alexandria, VA: ASCD.

About the Authors

James H. Stronge is the Heritage Professor of Education, a distinguished professorship in the Educational Policy, Planning, and Leadership Area at the College of William and Mary in Williamsburg, Virginia. He teaches master's and doctoral courses within the School of Education's Educational Policy, Planning, and Leadership Program. He is also the president of Stronge and Associates, an educational consulting group that focuses on teacher and leader effectiveness.

Prior to coming to William and Mary, Stronge taught at Bradley University. He has also been a teacher, counselor, and district-level administrator. He holds a doctorate in educational administration and planning from the University of Alabama at Tuscaloosa.

Stronge's research interests include policy and practice related to teacher quality and effectiveness and teacher and administrator evaluation. He has worked with numerous state departments of education, school districts, and national and international educational organizations to design and implement evaluation systems for teachers, administrators, and support personnel. Recently, he completed work on new teacher and principal evaluation systems for U.S. schools in South America, and launched a project for principals in 2012 in conjunction with the Association of American Schools in South America. Stronge has presented his research at national and international conferences and conducted workshops for U.S. and international educational organizations. Among his current research projects are comparative studies of national award-winning teachers in the United States and China.

Stronge has authored, coauthored, or edited 23 books and more than 100 articles, chapters, and technical reports. His most recent books include *Effective Teachers = Student Achievement: What the Research Says* (2010) and *Evaluating What Good Teachers Do: Eight Research-Based Standards for Assessing Teacher Excellence* (2010). His 1994 book, *Educating Homeless Children and Adolescents: Evaluating Policy and Practice,* received the Outstanding Academic Book Award from the American Library Association.

Stronge was a founding member of the board of directors for the Consortium for Research on Educational Accountability and Teacher Evaluation. In 2011, he was honored with the Frank E. Flora Lamp of Knowledge Award, presented by the Virginia Association of Secondary School Principals for "bringing honor to the profession" and a "record of outstanding contributions." He was selected as the 2012 recipient of the Millman Award from CREATE in recognition of his work in the field of teacher and administrator evaluation. Stronge can be reached by e-mail at james.stronge@strongeandassociates.com.

Xianxuan Xu received her doctorate from the College of William and Mary's Educational Policy, Planning, and Leadership Program. She is currently working as a postdoctoral research associate for a statewide teacher evaluation project funded by the Virginia Department of Education and based at the College of William and Mary. Her research interests include teacher effectiveness, teacher and principal evaluation, and international comparative analyses of teacher qualities. She has presented findings of her research at national conferences, including those of the American Educational Research Association, the University Council for Educational Administration, and the National Evaluation Institute.

Lauri M. Leeper is a postdoctoral research associate at the College of William and Mary and an educational consultant with Stronge and Associates. In the latter capacity, she works with state agencies and school districts on teacher and administrator evaluation systems. Her current research interests include teacher and administrator evaluation, teacher effectiveness, teacher leadership, and effective reading comprehension instruction. She is a former middle school and elementary school teacher, a certified library media specialist, and a certified reading specialist. She has presented at national-, state-, and local-level conferences on topics including teacher evaluation, closing the achievement gap, effective schools, information literacy, inquiry-based learning, and curriculum design. Leeper received her doctoral degree in Educational Policy, Planning, and Leadership from the College of William and Mary.

Virginia C. Tonneson is the vice president of Stronge and Associates and a postdoctoral research associate at the College of William and Mary. In these capacities, she works with regional, state, and international agencies as well as individual school districts to design and implement teacher, educational specialist, and administrator evaluation systems. Ginny was in the first class of women to graduate from the U.S. Air Force Academy, and served in the Air Force for over 20 years. She has remained active in the education of cadets, speaking in various forums about leadership and character development. She has taught at the elementary through graduate levels and has been a higher education administrator. She has presented at national-, state-, and local-level conferences in the areas of leadership, mathematics, and gifted education. Her current areas of research include teacher leadership as well as teacher and leader effectiveness. Her work has been published in both books and peer-reviewed journals. Ginny received her doctoral degree in Educational Policy, Planning, Leadership from the College of William and Mary.